Finding Me

OrangeBooks Publication

1st Floor, Rajhans Arcade, Mall Road, Kohka, Bhilai, Chhattisgarh 490020

Website: **www.orangebooks.in**

© Copyright, 2024, Author

All rights reserved. No part of this book may be reproduced, stored in a retrieval system, or transmitted, in any form by any means, electronic, mechanical, magnetic, optical, chemical, manual, photocopying, recording or otherwise, without the prior written consent of its writer.

First Edition, 2024

ISBN: 978-93-6554-125-0

FINDING ME

EMBRACING SPIRITUALITY IN STUDENT LIFE

HARISH TOLANI

OrangeBooks Publication
www.orangebooks.in

This Book is Dedicated To

To the dreamers and doers, the students destined to change the world and shape a brilliant future.

And to the extraordinary teachers, the guiding stars who are more than educators – friends, mentors, and navigators on the journey to greatness.

Content

First Words 1
Purpose of Book 5
My Journey 9
What is Spirituality 15
Why Spirituality Matters For Students 22

Finding Light (A Teenager's Journey Through Darkness) 29

    Chapter - 1: The Beginning of The Storm 30

    Chapter - 2: A Glimmer of Hope 38

    Chapter - 3: The Path To Recovery 43

The Student's World 47

The Path Unseen "A Tale of Friendship And Spiritual Awakening" 57

    Chapter - 1: The Bold Spirit 58

    Chapter - 2: Echoes of Solitude 61

    Chapter - 3: Revival 71

Practices For Spiritual Growth 78

    Mindfulness And Meditation 86

    Gratitude And Journaling 90

    Nature And Solitude 94

    Faith In God 99

From Rebel To Serenity "A Journey of Spiritual Transformation" 104

    Chapter - 1: The Charismatic Rebel 105

Chapter - 2: The Price Of Rebellion 109

Chapter - 3: Guiding Light.. 115

Bhagavad Geeta "A Timeless Wisdom" 123

Harish Sir's Gita Insights Navigating Student Life 129

   Mastering Actions: Beyond Results.................... 130
   The Catalyst For Self-Discipline 136
   Embracing Responsibility 142
   Faith - Beyond Doubt.. 146
   Ride of Life... 152
   Multi-Thinking And The Art of Balance 158
   The Balance of The World:................................. 163
   The Power of Right Actions 163
   Echoes of Intent: Navigating Life's Choices 169
   Discovering Divinity Within 175
   Garbage In, Garbage Out.................................... 181
   Finding The Perfect Blend of The
   Gunas (Qualities)... 190
   Be A God/Good Person.. 197
   Rediscovering Identity: Beyond Caste
   And Labels.. 203

Discovering Wisdom: 209

The Relevance of The Bhagavad Gita 209

Final Words: 212

Guiding Youth Toward Wisdom And Purpose 212

A Gratitude Note 221

First Words

Imagine navigating the wild, exhilarating rollercoaster ride that is high school with a trusty guide by your side, one that doesn't just help you ace your exams but also helps you discover the real you. That's what this book aims to be—a companion on your journey through the most formative years of your life, steering you towards a deeper understanding of yourself and the world around you.

Why This Book?

In today's fast-paced, hyper-connected world, being a student comes with its own unique set of challenges. There are academic pressures, social dynamics, extracurricular commitments, and of course, the constant buzz of social media. Amidst this whirlwind, finding moments of calm and clarity can seem like an impossible task. This is where spirituality steps in, offering a sanctuary of peace, purpose, and perspective.

As a teacher, I've had the privilege of walking this path alongside countless students. I've seen first-hand the transformative power of spirituality. It's not about adhering to a strict set of rules or following a particular religion—it's about finding what resonates with you and helps you grow into the best version of yourself.

My own journey with spirituality began as a quest for balance and meaning amidst the chaos of life. What I discovered was a treasure trove of wisdom, practices, and insights that not only enhanced my life but also profoundly impacted my teaching. I've woven these experiences and lessons into this book, hoping to share the joy and serenity I've found.

You might wonder why my students call me "Chikoo Bhaiya" instead of the more formal "Harish Sir." The reason is simple: we share a bond that goes beyond the classroom. I'm not just their teacher; I'm their friend, philosopher, and guide. "Chikoo Bhaiya" reflects the unique connection we have, one that is rooted in trust, mutual respect, and genuine care. This book is an extension of that relationship, designed to guide you with the same warmth and understanding.

What to Expect

"Finding Me - Embracing Spirituality in Student Life" is designed to be your roadmap to inner peace and self-discovery. It's packed with practical advice, relatable stories, and engaging exercises. Here's a sneak peek of what you'll find inside:

- **Understanding Spirituality:** Unravelling what spirituality truly means and how it can enrich your life.

- **The Student's World:** Navigating the highs and lows of student life with a spiritual compass.

- **Practices for Spiritual Growth:** From mindfulness and meditation to gratitude and journaling, discover practices that resonate with you.

- **Building Positive Habits:** Crafting routines and setting intentions that support your spiritual journey.

- **Connecting with Others:** Cultivating empathy, compassion, and community spirit.

- **Overcoming Obstacles: Building** resilience and handling negativity with grace.

- **Incorporating Spirituality into Academics:** Enhancing your studies and ethical understanding through spiritual principles.
- **Stories and Anecdotes:** Real-life examples and inspirational tales to motivate and inspire you.

A Journey Worth Taking

This book is more than just a collection of chapters—it's a journey we'll embark on together. You'll laugh, you might cry, and you'll definitely learn a lot about yourself. So, buckle up, keep an open mind, and get ready to dive into the enriching world of spirituality.

Whether you're seeking a sense of calm amidst the chaos, looking to foster deeper connections, or simply curious about what spirituality has to offer, this book is for you. Together, let's explore the path to inner growth and unlock the extraordinary potential that lies within you.

Welcome aboard, fellow traveller. Let's embark on this adventure and uncover the magic of spirituality in student life.

Warm Regards,
- Harish Tolani (Chikoo Bhaiya)

Purpose of Book

In the hustle and bustle of student life, amidst exams, social pressures, and the constant quest for identity, there lies a quieter journey—one of introspection, discovery, and inner peace. This book is your guide to navigating that journey with grace and understanding.

What does it mean to be spiritual? At its core, spirituality transcends religious affiliations and rituals. It's about connecting with a deeper sense of purpose, finding meaning in life's challenges, and nurturing a sense of inner peace. Take, for example, A.C. Bhakti Vedanta Swami Prabhupada, whose profound spiritual journey led him to introduce Vedic teachings and practices to the Western world. Against all odds, he spread the message of peace and devotion, inspiring countless individuals to embrace spirituality as a way of life.

Mahatma Gandhi's commitment to nonviolence and truth was rooted in his deep spiritual beliefs. Despite facing immense obstacles, his spiritual resilience guided India to independence.

For Oprah Winfrey, spirituality has been a guiding force in her life and career. She often speaks of her daily practice of gratitude and meditation, which helps her maintain balance and clarity amidst her demanding schedule.

In today's world, there are several prominent figures who embody the principles of spirituality and self-discovery, resonating deeply with today's youth

Sadhguru (Jaggi Vasudev), a spiritual leader, yogi, and founder of the Isha Foundation, Sadhguru's teachings on inner engineering and holistic well-being have captivated millions worldwide. His approach combines ancient wisdom with contemporary insights, making spirituality accessible and relevant to modern-day challenges.

Malala Yousafzai, known for her advocacy of girls' education and human rights, Malala's courage and resilience in the face of adversity reflect a deep inner strength rooted in her spiritual beliefs. Her journey from surviving a Taliban assassination attempt to becoming the youngest Nobel Prize laureate is a testament to the power of faith and determination.

Let me share with you a story—a tale of how life's unexpected twists led me to where I am today. As a young Chartered Accountant, I embarked on a journey that was meant to be a testament to hard work and ambition. The path to becoming a CA was paved with emotional turmoil, tragic setbacks, and endless mental exhaustion. Yet, despite achieving this milestone, I found myself at a crossroads.

Imagine standing at the intersection of two diverging paths: one leading to a prestigious corporate career in finance, and the other, unexpectedly, to the front of a classroom filled with eager schoolchildren. Many questioned my decision—to trade spreadsheets and boardrooms for textbooks and chalkboards seemed unfathomable. It was a dilemma that tugged at my heart and tested my resolve.

In those moments of uncertainty, spirituality became my guiding light. It wasn't about choosing between two careers; it was about aligning my passion with purpose. Teaching, I realized, wasn't just a profession—it was a calling. It offered me a chance to connect deeply with young minds, to inspire and nurture future leaders. And amidst the chaos of balancing both worlds, spirituality provided me with the clarity and resilience to forge ahead.

This book is more than just theory; it's a practical handbook for integrating spirituality into your daily life. From mindfulness practices to ethical considerations, each chapter offers insights and exercises designed to foster personal growth and resilience.

Whether you're new to spirituality or have been on this path for some time, each chapter invites you to reflect, engage, and take practical steps toward inner peace and fulfilment. Embrace it as a companion—a friend who understands your journey and encourages your growth.

So, with the hope that this book inspires and empower you to discover your own path to inner growth, let's embark on this journey together. Open your heart and mind to the possibilities that spirituality holds for you.

My Journey

I am Harish Tolani, popularly known as 'Chikoo Bhaiya'—a name affectionately given to me by my students. Though I can't pinpoint exactly when or how it happened, I embraced it with an open heart and have kept it close to myself.

As a kid, I wasn't very confident; I was a simple, introverted child. But deep inside, I harbored a lot of emotions and believed I had the potential to do great things. I always imagined myself as the hero of my own story. In movies, the hero faces difficulties, hardships, heartbreaks, and setbacks but still pushes through to survive and succeed. I related my situations—my lack of confidence and problems—to those of the heroes, seeing myself in a similar struggle for survival and success.

Growing up as the eldest child in a lower-middle-class family with an orthodox environment, I was often restricted in what I could do. But you can't restrict thoughts. I wasn't very good in academics, nor was I physically fit or talented in sports. I often felt overshadowed by the school toppers and the athletic stars. My classmates would bully me, and I envied them—their cool demeanour, their confidence, the way they effortlessly talked with girls. Despite these challenges, I kept my dreams alive. Slowly and gradually, I fell and stood up again, grappling with the fear of losing and the fear of the unknown. Somehow, I managed to rise above these challenges, drawing strength from my faith in Lord Krishna. His teachings and stories became a source of inspiration and guidance for me.

Completing my Chartered Accountancy course was a significant milestone. It was a journey fraught with difficulty, exhaustion, and mental strain. During a time when emotions run high and it's hard to distinguish right from wrong, I faced constant fear and uncertainty. It's an age where there's both a fear of the Unknown and an urge to live in the moment. I was always in a dilemma about what to do and what not to do. Spirituality helped me navigate these decisions. Whether my choices were right or wrong, taking a decision between two right options is a task in itself.

The journey of dilemmas didn't end there. After completing CA, I faced the challenge of finding employment. The dilemma was ever-present: choosing between job offers, deciding on marriage, having kids, dealing with career setbacks, and finding my footing again. Balancing everything was tough. Yet, spirituality helped me make decisions, stay strong, and most importantly, meet myself.

In one particularly challenging phase, I was torn between continuing my profession as a Chartered Accountant or transitioning fully into teaching. It was getting increasingly tough to juggle both. Imagine the scene: late nights with financial statements, followed by early mornings with eager students. I found myself at a crossroads, overwhelmed by the stress and the growing discontent in my heart. One night, after a particularly gruelling day, I sat alone with my thoughts. The silence was both deafening and comforting. It was then that I turned to spirituality and my faith in Lord Krishna. Through meditation and introspection, I found clarity. I realized that my true calling was to teach, to inspire young minds. That decision, though difficult, brought me immense peace and fulfilment.

Just as I found my path through spirituality, many well-known personalities have also turned to it to find direction and peace. Take, for example, Virat Kohli. Known for his aggression on the cricket field and his intense dedication, Kohli faced a tumultuous period in his career. His performance was inconsistent, and the pressures of fame and expectations weighed heavily on him. It was during this phase that he embraced spirituality. Meditation and mindfulness practices transformed his approach to life and the game. Kohli attributes his improved focus, emotional balance, and renewed energy to his spiritual practices, which have since become an integral part of his daily routine.

Similarly, Malala Yousafzai, the youngest Nobel laureate, drew immense strength from her spiritual beliefs. After surviving a Taliban assassination attempt, her faith and resilience guided her to become a global advocate for girls' education. Her journey from a small village in Pakistan to the halls of the United Nations is a testament to the power of spiritual strength in overcoming adversity.

Steve Jobs, the co-founder of Apple, is another example. In the 1970s, Jobs travelled to India in search of spiritual enlightenment. His experiences and the teachings he encountered deeply influenced his life and work. Jobs often credited his spiritual journey with providing him the clarity and focus needed to revolutionize the tech industry. His minimalist design philosophy and emphasis on intuition were direct reflections of his spiritual insights.

Indian youth icon Ranveer Allahbadia, also known as Beer Biceps, has inspired millions through his journey into spirituality. Once a fitness enthusiast and entrepreneur facing immense pressure and burnout, Ranveer turned to spirituality to find balance. Practices like meditation, yoga, and reading spiritual texts transformed his life. Today, he shares his experiences with his audience, emphasizing the importance of mental and spiritual well-being alongside physical health.

These examples reflect how spirituality and faith in a higher power can provide a foundation of strength and clarity, even in the most challenging times. But it's not just famous personalities who face dilemmas. Everyday students, too, grapple with significant challenges and decisions.

Consider the case of Rohan, one of my very bright students torn between his passion for music and his parents' expectations of a career in engineering. The pressure to perform academically while nurturing his creative side left him in a constant state of anxiety. Through mindfulness practices and his faith in a higher power, Rohan found a way to balance both worlds, achieving academic success while still pursuing his love for music.

Then there's Priya, my sweet little ever smiling student, who struggled with severe exam anxiety. The fear of failure loomed over her, affecting her performance and self-esteem. By incorporating meditation and breathing exercises into her daily routine, and maintaining faith in the Supreme, Priya managed to calm her mind, improve her concentration, and approach exams with a new found confidence.

A particularly inspiring example is Bhavna, one of my brightest students. Her family was not financially strong, but she was a good and promising student. She faced numerous challenges, from financial constraints to societal pressures. However, Bhavna kept her faith and persevered against all odds. Spirituality played a significant role in her journey. It helped her stay focused, resilient, and optimistic. Today, she is a Chartered Accountant, just like I am. Bhavna's journey from a struggling student to a successful professional is a testament to the power of faith, hard work, and spiritual grounding.

These stories, both of well-known figures and everyday students, highlight the profound impact spirituality and faith can have on navigating life's dilemmas. It's a journey of self-discovery, resilience, and inner peace that I, too, have experienced.

Each step in my journey has been a blend of struggle and triumph, guided by an inner resilience nurtured through spirituality and faith in Lord Krishna. I've learned that life's dilemmas are constant, but with a spiritual compass, you can navigate them with grace.

This journey has shaped me into the person I am today—Chikoo Bhaiya, a teacher, a guide, and a friend to my students.

What is Spirituality

Spirituality is a word that often conjures up images of monks meditating on mountaintops or people chanting in dimly lit rooms filled with incense. But let's simplify things a bit. Spirituality is about connecting with something bigger than ourselves. It's about finding purpose, meaning, and understanding in life, whether that's through religion, nature, art, or even science. It's like having a GPS for the soul, helping us navigate through life's ups and downs.

Spirituality is a deeply personal and often misunderstood concept. At its core, spirituality involves a sense of connection to something greater than ourselves. This connection could be to a higher power, the universe, or simply the collective human experience. It's about seeking meaning, purpose, and inner peace. While some may find spirituality in religion, others might discover it through nature, art, or even science. Spirituality is not about following a strict set of rules but about exploring and understanding the deeper aspects of life.

Some may find that their spiritual life is intricately linked to their association with a church, temple, mosque, or synagogue. Others may pray or find comfort in a personal relationship with God or a higher power. Still others seek meaning through their connections to nature or art. Like your sense of purpose, your personal definition of spirituality may change throughout your life, adapting to your own experiences and relationships. For many, spirituality is connected to large questions about life and identity, such as:

- Am I a good person?
- What is the meaning of my suffering?
- What is my connection to the world around me?
- Do things happen for a reason?
- How can I live my life in the best way possible?

Different Perspectives on Spirituality

The Religious Perspective

For many, spirituality is deeply intertwined with religion. It's about following the teachings of a higher power, engaging in prayer, rituals, and community worship. Think of it as a structured way to connect with the divine, like having a regular schedule to meet your spiritual guru (who just happens to be God).

The Secular Perspective

Others see spirituality as a more personal and individualized journey. It's about inner peace, self-awareness, and personal growth. This perspective doesn't necessarily involve a deity but focuses on being mindful, living in the moment, and understanding one's place in the universe. It's like being your own life coach, but with a touch of zen.

The Philosophical Perspective

Some folks dive into spirituality through philosophy, pondering life's big questions: Why are we here? What's the meaning of life? Is there an afterlife? These deep thinkers might not meditate or pray, but they explore spirituality through intellectual exploration and ethical living. Imagine a book club where the reading list includes Plato, Rumi, and Oprah Winfrey.

Simplifying Spirituality

To break it down further, let's use a fun analogy. Imagine life is like a gigantic, chaotic shopping mall. Spirituality is the mall map and directory that helps you find the best stores, avoid the crowds, and maybe even discover a hidden food court with the best nachos in town. Here's how:

Finding Purpose

Like finding a job you love or a hobby that makes you forget to check your phone. It's that "Aha!" moment when you realize what you're passionate about.

Connecting with Others

Building meaningful relationships and communities. It's that feeling of being part of something bigger, whether it's a family, a club, or a random group of people who also love knitting cat sweaters.

Inner Peace

Finding calm amidst chaos. It's like the mental version of sinking into a warm bubble bath after a long day, but without the wrinkly fingers.

Spirituality is a multifaceted concept that has been interpreted in various ways by different thinkers, philosophers, and leaders across the world. Let's explore some profound definitions of spirituality as given by renowned Indian and international personalities.

"Spirituality is the essence of all religions. It is the pursuit of truth and the quest for an understanding of the divine."

- Mahatma Gandhi

For Gandhi, spirituality was about seeking truth and understanding the divine presence in all aspects of life. His approach to spirituality was deeply rooted in non-violence, compassion, and self-discipline. He believed that true spirituality transcended religious boundaries and was about living a life of integrity and service to others.

"Spirituality is the manifestation of the divine within us. It is realizing our potential and expressing it in our thoughts, words, and actions."

- Swami Vivekananda

Swami Vivekananda viewed spirituality as the realization and expression of the divine qualities within each individual. He emphasized the importance of self-realization, inner strength, and the development of character. According to him, spirituality was about recognizing our true nature and living in accordance with it.

"Spirituality is the awakening of the soul to the reality of the spirit. It is the journey towards a higher consciousness and the transformation of our nature."

- Sri Aurobindo

Sri Aurobindo's definition of spirituality focused on the awakening of the soul and the journey towards higher consciousness. He believed in the transformative power of spirituality to elevate human nature and bring about a deeper understanding of the universe and our place in it.

> *"Spirituality is not about looking up or down; it's about looking in. It is a way to explore the ultimate nature of who you are."*
>
> *- Sadhguru (Jaggi Vasudev)*

Sadhguru emphasizes the inward journey of spirituality, where one seeks to understand their true self. He believes that spirituality is about exploring and realizing the ultimate nature of our existence beyond the physical and mental dimensions.

> *"My religion consists of a humble admiration of the illimitable superior spirit who reveals himself in the slight details we are able to perceive with our frail and feeble mind."*
>
> *- Albert Einstein*

Einstein's spirituality was rooted in a profound sense of awe and wonder at the universe. He believed in a higher power that manifested through the intricate workings of the cosmos. For him, spirituality was about recognizing the limitations of human understanding and appreciating the mysteries of existence.

> *"Spirituality is concerned with those qualities of the human spirit—such as love, compassion, patience, tolerance, forgiveness, contentment, a sense of responsibility, and a sense of harmony—that bring happiness to both self and others."*
>
> *- Dalai Lama*

The Dalai Lama's view of spirituality focuses on the development of positive human qualities. He emphasizes that spirituality is about cultivating virtues that contribute to personal happiness and the well-being of others. It's about fostering inner peace and harmony in our interactions with the world.

"Spirituality is to be in the present moment, to be fully present and aware of the now."

- Eckhart Tolle

Eckhart Tolle's concept of spirituality revolves around mindfulness and presence. He believes that true spirituality is about being fully engaged in the present moment, free from the distractions of past regrets and future anxieties. It's about experiencing life as it unfolds and finding peace in the now.

"Spirituality is about compassion and love. It is about recognizing the divine in each person and serving them as we would serve God."

- Mother Teresa

Mother Teresa viewed spirituality as an expression of love and compassion. For her, spirituality was about seeing the divine presence in every individual and serving humanity selflessly. She believed that by helping others, we connect with the divine and fulfil our spiritual purpose.

Why Spirituality Matters for Students

In today's fast-paced, digitally driven world, compassion is more important than ever. But what exactly is compassion? It's more than just feeling sorry for someone. It means truly understanding what others are going through and wanting to help ease their pain. Unfortunately, social media often makes things worse by encouraging comparison, judgment, and shallow interactions. This can lead to a lack of genuine empathy and kindness, making many of us feel isolated and disconnected.

Here's where spirituality comes in. It can help us develop compassion as a key part of our lives. When you practice mindfulness and self-reflection, you become more aware of your own feelings and those of others. This awareness helps you naturally recognize and understand the struggles your friends and classmates might be facing, fostering real empathy and kindness.

Imagine a school where everyone practices compassion. It would be a place where each of you feels valued and understood. Healthy relationships would thrive, bullying and social exclusion would decrease, and overall well-being would improve. When you experience compassion, you're more likely to help others, offer support when it's needed, and contribute positively to your community.

Moreover, compassion can protect you from the loneliness that often comes from shallow social media interactions. By building genuine connections based on empathy and kindness, spirituality helps you become more resilient and emotionally intelligent. This not only helps you grow as a person but also prepares you to be compassionate leaders and responsible members of society.

Let's break it down that why actually spirituality matters for students:

1. Coping with Stress and Anxiety

Student life today is marked by a whirlwind of challenges: relentless exams, constant peer pressure, looming deadlines, and now, the ever-present stress of social media and self-expectations. With Instagram likes dictating self-worth and other social media trends shaping social acceptance, students face a digital landscape that amplifies anxiety and self-doubt. Spirituality steps in as a guiding light, offering invaluable tools such as meditation, deep breathing exercises, and mindfulness practices. These tools aren't just remedies; they are lifelines that help students cultivate inner peace and resilience. By practicing these techniques, students can effectively manage the dual pressures of academic demands and social expectations, navigating through the noise with greater calm, clarity, and emotional stability.

2. Building Emotional Intelligence

Spirituality encourages introspection and self-reflection, key components of emotional intelligence. Students who engage in spiritual practices often develop a heightened awareness of their emotions, enabling them to navigate relationships, setbacks, and personal challenges with empathy and maturity.

3. Fostering Compassionate Connections

In today's fast-paced and digitally driven world, the cultivation of compassion among students is more crucial than ever. Compassion goes beyond mere sympathy; it involves understanding and empathizing with others' emotions and experiences, and actively seeking to alleviate their suffering. Unfortunately, societal trends and the prevalence of social media often contribute to a culture of comparison, judgment, and superficial interactions among young people. This can lead to a lack of genuine empathy and kindness, fostering an environment where students may feel isolated or disconnected.

Spirituality offers a powerful antidote to this trend by emphasizing the importance of compassion as a foundational principle. When students embrace spiritual practices that encourage compassion, such as mindfulness and self-reflection, they develop a deeper awareness of their own emotions and those of others. This heightened sensitivity allows them to recognize the struggles and challenges faced by their peers, fostering empathy and kindness naturally.

In a school setting, a culture of compassion creates a supportive and inclusive environment where every student feels valued and understood. It promotes healthy relationships, reduces instances of bullying and social exclusion, and enhances overall well-being. Students who experience compassion are more likely to reach out to others in need, offer support during difficult times, and contribute positively to their community.

Moreover, compassion acts as a shield against the negative effects of social isolation and loneliness that can arise from superficial social interactions. By fostering genuine connections based on empathy and kindness, spirituality helps students build resilience and emotional intelligence. This not only benefits their personal growth but also prepares them to become compassionate leaders and responsible members of society.

Therefore, integrating spiritual principles that emphasize compassion into education is essential for nurturing a generation of students who are not only academically successful but also empathetic, kind-hearted, and capable of creating a more compassionate world. It lays the foundation for a school culture where compassion is celebrated and practiced daily, ensuring that no student feels alone or unsupported on their journey through education and beyond.

4. Finding Purpose and Meaning

Amidst the pursuit of academic and career goals, students often grapple with questions of purpose and meaning. Spirituality offers a framework for exploring these existential questions, helping students align their ambitions with their values and aspirations. This clarity of purpose fuels motivation and resilience in the face of setbacks.

Integrating Spirituality into Student Life
1. Mindfulness Practices
Practice mindfulness through guided meditation sessions or simple breathing exercises. This helps them develop focus, reduce anxiety, and enhance overall well-being.

2. Cultivating Gratitude
Have a gratitude journals or activities where students reflect on things, they are grateful for each day. Gratitude fosters a positive mindset and resilience in the face of challenges.

3. Community and Service
Engage students in community service projects that align with their values and interests. Serving others cultivates empathy, instils a sense of responsibility, and reinforces the principles of compassion central to spirituality.

4. Reflective Exercises
Incorporate reflective exercises into classroom activities or extracurricular programs. Encourage students to journal about their personal growth, experiences, and insights gained through spiritual practices.

Spirituality empowers students to cultivate inner strength, emotional well-being, and a sense of purpose amidst the complexities of academic and personal life. By integrating spiritual principles into education, schools can nurture holistic development, resilience, and compassionate leadership among students. Ultimately, spirituality provides a transformative framework for students to thrive academically, socially, and emotionally, preparing them to lead fulfilling lives with empathy and in conclusion, spirituality is a versatile and personal journey that can bring profound benefits to our lives. Whether through religious practices, personal growth, philosophical exploration, or simply being present, spirituality helps us navigate life's challenges and find meaning in our experiences. So, take a deep breath, find your inner compass, and embark on your own spiritual adventure. Who knows what wonderful discoveries await you?

Finding Light
(A Teenager's Journey Through Darkness)

Chapter - 1
The Beginning of the Storm

Rohan Kapoor was a lively sixteen-year-old, always the centre of laughter and fun. With his bright eyes and infectious smile, he had a knack for making everyone around him feel at ease. He was the life of the party, known for his witty jokes and playful pranks. Rohan's world revolved around his close-knit group of friends, his loving family, and his passion for cricket.

His best friends, Arjun, Priya, and Sameer, were like his second family. They spent countless hours together, whether it was playing cricket in the local park, binge-watching movies, or simply hanging out at their favourite cafe, sipping on cold coffee and discussing everything under the sun.

"Hey Rohan, did you finish the math homework?" Priya asked one afternoon, twirling her hair nervously.

"Finish? I haven't even started!" Rohan replied with a grin. "I'll just wing it in class tomorrow."

Arjun laughed, "Classic Rohan! Always the last-minute warrior."

Despite his carefree attitude towards studies, Rohan was surprisingly good at managing to scrape through with decent grades. He wasn't the top of the class, but he wasn't at the bottom either. He was happy being in the middle, enjoying life as it came.

At home, Rohan shared a warm relationship with his parents and his younger sister, Riya. His mother, Neha, was the glue that held the family together, always making sure everyone was taken care of. His father, Raj, was a strict but loving man who worked long hours as an accountant.

"Dad, can we go to the cricket match this weekend?" Rohan asked one evening at the dinner table.

"Rohan, you know I've got work," Raj replied, looking up from his plate. "But I'll try to make time."

Riya piped up, "I want to go too! Rohan, teach me how to play cricket!"

Rohan chuckled, "Sure, little champ. You'll be the best bowler in no time."

Life was good for Rohan, filled with laughter, friends, and the occasional family squabble. However, as the months went by, the pressures of school and life began to mount. The carefree days started to fade as Rohan struggled to keep up with the increasing demands of academics and the unspoken expectations from his family.

He found himself spending more time alone, his mind a whirlpool of worries about grades, college admissions, and the future. The pressure to perform academically began to weigh heavily on him, and his once vibrant personality started to dim.

One evening, after a particularly gruelling day at school, Rohan sat quietly in his room. His phone buzzed with messages from friends, but he ignored them. The familiar laughter and joy felt like distant memories.

"Rohan, dinner's ready," his mother called from the kitchen.

"I'm not hungry, Mom," he replied, staring at the ceiling.

His mother walked in, concerned. "Are you okay, beta? You've been so quiet lately."

"I'm fine, Mom. Just tired," he muttered, forcing a smile.

Neha sighed, sensing something was off but not knowing how to reach out to him. Rohan's mind was a storm of thoughts and emotions he couldn't express, a far cry from the carefree boy he once was.

The pressures of social media also began to take their toll. Scrolling through Instagram, he saw friends posting about their achievements, vacations, and perfect lives. It made him feel inadequate, as if he was falling behind in some invisible race.

"Why can't I have it all together like them?" he thought to himself, the weight of comparison pressing down on him.

Despite the love and support around him, Rohan felt increasingly isolated. He withdrew from his friends, skipped cricket practice, and spent more time alone, lost in a sea of self-doubt and anxiety.

The breaking point came during a conversation with Arjun after school one day. They were sitting on the steps outside the building, watching the sunset.

"Hey, Rohan, are you okay? You've been so distant lately," Arjun said, his voice filled with concern.

Rohan sighed, staring at the horizon. "I don't know, man. Everything just feels so overwhelming. The pressure from school, social media, everything. I feel like I'm drowning."

Arjun put a hand on his shoulder. "You're not alone, you know? We all feel that way sometimes. But you can't just shut everyone out. Talk to us. We're here for you."

Rohan looked at Arjun, a mix of frustration and sadness in his eyes. "It's not that easy, Arjun. Sometimes I feel like no one really gets it. I don't even know if I get it."

Arjun gave him a reassuring squeeze. "Just remember, you're not in this alone. And maybe... maybe you need to find something that can help you cope. Something more than just hanging out and playing cricket."

Rohan nodded, feeling a flicker of hope. "Yeah, maybe you're right."

As Rohan's world became more turbulent, he realized he was heading into a storm he wasn't prepared for. The boy who once brought light into every room was now struggling to find a spark within himself. Little did he know, this journey through the storm would lead him to a place of profound transformation and self-discovery.

Rohan's descent into the darkest period of his life didn't happen overnight. It was a gradual build-up of stress, pressure, and overwhelming emotions. But there was one incident that pushed him over the edge, an event that marked the lowest point in his journey.

It all started with the annual school talent show. Every year, students showcased their talents, and it was a highly anticipated event. Rohan, who was once the life of the party, had always participated, be it with a stand-up comedy act or a skit with his friends. This year, however, he felt too overwhelmed to join in.

"Hey Rohan, are you performing this year?" Sameer asked during lunch one day.

Rohan shook his head. "Nah, I don't think so. I have too much on my plate."

Arjun, who was always the motivator, chimed in, "Come on, Rohan! It won't be the same without you. You always bring the house down."

But Rohan just couldn't bring himself to do it. The thought of standing on stage and making people laugh felt impossible. He was too consumed by his own struggles.

The talent show came and went, and Rohan watched from the side-lines as his friends took the stage. They did well, but it wasn't the same without Rohan's energy. After the show, his friends tried to cheer him up, but he felt more isolated than ever.

A few days later, the school buzzed with excitement about the upcoming cricket tournament. Rohan, who had always been a key player, found himself unable to focus during practice. His mind was elsewhere, and it showed in his performance.

"Rohan, what's going on? You're off your game," the coach said, pulling him aside after practice.

Rohan shrugged, avoiding eye contact. "I don't know, coach. Just a lot on my mind."

The coach sighed. "You need to get it together, Rohan. The team is counting on you."

Despite the coach's pep talk, Rohan couldn't shake off the weight on his shoulders. The tournament day arrived, and Rohan's performance was disastrous. He missed catches, fumbled with the bat, and the team lost. It was a crushing defeat, and Rohan felt responsible.

As if things couldn't get worse, the next blow came from social media. A video clip of Rohan's mistakes during the match went viral among the students. It was meant to be funny, but it quickly turned into a source of ridicule. Memes and jokes about Rohan's performance flooded his Instagram feed.

"Look at this loser!" one caption read.

"Rohan the Great Fumbler!" another post mocked.

Rohan tried to brush it off, but the constant notifications and messages were relentless. His friends tried to support him, but even they couldn't shield him from the onslaught.

One evening, while scrolling through the endless stream of hurtful comments, Rohan's phone buzzed with a message from Arjun.

"Hey, bro. Don't let this get to you. People can be cruel. We're here for you."

Rohan stared at the message, feeling a mix of anger and despair. He appreciated Arjun's support, but the damage was done. He felt humiliated and defeated.

The next day at school, things came to a head. Walking down the hallway, Rohan could feel the stares and hear the whispers. He tried to ignore them, but it was impossible. As he approached his locker, he found a note taped to it.

"Quit the team, loser."

Rohan's hands trembled as he ripped the note off and crumpled it in his fist. He felt a surge of anger and sadness, but more than anything, he felt alone.

He skipped classes that day, hiding in the library where he hoped to find some solace. But the silence only amplified his thoughts. He wondered how things had spiralled so out of control. He questioned his worth and whether he would ever feel like himself again.

In the midst of this darkness, Rohan's relationship with his family also suffered. He became withdrawn, barely speaking to his parents or sister. His mother, Neha, noticed the change and tried to reach out.

"Rohan, talk to me. What's going on?" she asked one evening, sitting beside him on the couch.

"I'm fine, Mom. Just leave me alone," he replied, his voice void of the usual warmth.

Neha's heart ached for her son, but she didn't know how to help him. She prayed silently, hoping he would find his way out of this darkness.

Rohan's friends, too, were at a loss. They tried to include him in their activities, but he often declined, preferring to be alone. Priya, who had always been close to Rohan, decided to confront him.

"Rohan, this isn't you. We miss you," she said, her voice filled with concern.

"I miss me too, Priya. I just... I don't know how to fix this," Rohan admitted, his eyes brimming with tears.

Priya hugged him tightly. "You don't have to fix it alone. We're here for you, always."

Despite their words of encouragement, Rohan felt like he was sinking deeper into a pit of despair. He needed something more, something that could pull him out of this darkness and help him find his way again.

He felt an overwhelming sense of hopelessness. It was then that he remembered a book his grandmother had given him years ago, a book on spirituality that he had never bothered to read. Little did he know, the journey to finding himself would soon begin, guided by the unexpected path of spirituality.

Chapter - 2
A Glimmer of Hope

Rohan's life had turned into a series of grey, monotonous days. The once vibrant teenager was now a shadow of his former self, struggling to find meaning and direction. His schoolwork suffered, his relationships were strained, and he felt a growing emptiness within.

One afternoon, while rummaging through a dusty old trunk in his attic, Rohan stumbled upon an ancient-looking book. Its cover was worn, and the pages yellowed with age. The title read, "Bhagavad Gita." He had heard about this book before but never really paid much attention to it.

Curiosity piqued, Rohan took the book downstairs and began to flip through its pages. The text was dense, filled with verses written in Sanskrit, with translations and commentaries in English. It was challenging to comprehend, but something about the book intrigued him. He decided to seek help from someone who might understand it better.

His grandmother, Sushila, was known for her wisdom and deep spiritual insight. She was often seen meditating or reading scriptures, and Rohan admired her serene demeanour. He approached her one evening, the Bhagavad Gita in hand.

"Grandma, can you help me understand this book?" Rohan asked, sitting beside her on the veranda where she was enjoying her evening tea.

Sushila looked at the book and smiled gently. "Ah, the Bhagavad Gita. It's a profound scripture, Rohan. What made you pick it up?"

Rohan shrugged. "I don't know. I found it in the attic, and it seemed... interesting. But it's so hard to understand."

His grandmother nodded, her eyes twinkling with a mix of amusement and compassion. "The Bhagavad Gita is not just a book, Rohan. It's a guide to life. It's about understanding the self, duty, and the nature of the universe."

Rohan leaned in, intrigued. "Can you tell me more?"

Sushila closed her eyes for a moment, reciting a few verses from memory.

Chapter 2, Verse 47:

कर्मण्येवाधिकारस्ते मा फलेषु कदाचन ।
मा कर्मफलहेतुर्भूर्मा ते सङ्गोऽस्त्वकर्मणि ॥

"You have a right to perform your prescribed duties, but you are not entitled to the fruits of your actions. Never consider yourself to be the cause of the results of your activities, nor be attached to inaction."

She continued,

Chapter 2, Verse 13:

> देहिनोऽस्मिन्यथा देहे कौमारं यौवनं जरा |
> तथा देहान्तरप्राप्तिर्धीरस्तत्र न मुह्यति ||

Just as the soul experiences childhood, youth, and old age in this body, so too it will acquire another body. The wise are not deluded by this."

Rohan listened intently, trying to absorb the essence of the verses. "So, it's about doing your duty without worrying about the results?"

"Exactly," Sushila said, smiling. "The Bhagavad Gita teaches us to focus on our actions and leave the outcomes to the higher power. It reminds us that we are eternal souls, undergoing various experiences and learning from them."

One verse, in particular, caught Rohan's attention. Sushila recited it with a serene expression on her face.

Chapter 2, Verse 19:

> य एनं वेत्ति हन्तारं यश्चैनं मन्यते हतम् |
> उभौ तौ न विजानीतो नायं हन्ति न हन्यते ||

He who thinks that the soul kills, and he who thinks of it as killed, are both ignorant. The soul kills not, nor is it killed."

Rohan was captivated by this verse. The idea that the soul is eternal, beyond physical harm or death, resonated deeply with him. It offered a new perspective on life and its challenges.

"Grandma, this verse... it's so profound. It makes me think that maybe all these struggles and pains are just temporary. That there's something more beyond all this," Rohan said, his eyes reflecting a newfound spark.

Sushila nodded, her smile widening. "Exactly, Rohan. The Bhagavad Gita teaches us to rise above the transient nature of our problems and to understand our true, eternal self. It's a guide to inner peace and resilience."

Rohan felt a sense of peace wash over him. For the first time in weeks, he felt a glimmer of hope. He decided to delve deeper into the Bhagavad Gita, hoping to find answers to his questions and a way out of his turmoil.

As he started reading the book more earnestly, he found himself drawn to its teachings. The verses that once seemed complex now began to unfold layers of meaning. The wisdom of Lord Krishna's words to Arjuna on the battlefield resonated with Rohan, making him reflect on his own battles and struggles.

Rohan's curiosity about spirituality grew, and he started spending more time with his grandmother, discussing the Bhagavad Gita and its teachings. These conversations became a source of comfort and guidance, helping him navigate the storm within him.

Through these interactions, Rohan realized that the Bhagavad Gita was not just a book of religious teachings but a practical guide to life. Its timeless wisdom began to illuminate the path ahead, offering him tools to cope with his challenges and find inner strength.

The glimmer of hope that had ignited in Rohan's heart began to grow, slowly but surely transforming his outlook on life. He started to see his struggles not as insurmountable obstacles but as opportunities for growth and learning.

Chapter - 3
The Path to Recovery

Rohan's journey was far from over, but he now had a compass to guide him through the storm. The teachings of the Bhagavad Gita and his grandmother's wisdom provided him with the strength to face his fears and the clarity to find his true path.

Rohan's exploration of spirituality continued to evolve, guided by the teachings of the Bhagavad Gita and his deep conversations with his grandmother. Each discussion with her was like unlocking a new layer of wisdom that reshaped his understanding of life and purpose.

One evening, as they sat in the quiet comfort of her home, Rohan asked his grandmother about the nature of true happiness. She smiled gently, her eyes reflecting years of introspection and spiritual practice.

"Rohan," she began, "true happiness isn't found in chasing after temporary pleasures or material possessions. It resides within you, in the depths of your soul. The Bhagavad Gita teaches us that real joy comes from fulfilling our duties selflessly, without attachment to the results."

Her words resonated deeply with Rohan, who had often felt pressured to measure his worth by external achievements. He realized that happiness wasn't about what he could acquire, but about how he could contribute and grow as a person.

In addition to his study of the Bhagavad Gita, Rohan immersed himself in other spiritual texts that offered practical insights into daily living. Books on mindfulness and meditation techniques provided him with tools to cultivate inner peace and resilience. He learned about the power of gratitude, forgiveness, and self-awareness—qualities that became pillars of his spiritual practice.

Driven by his newfound understanding, Rohan adopted daily practices that nurtured his spiritual growth. Early morning meditation sessions became a sacred ritual, grounding him in the present moment and quieting the chatter of his mind. Yoga practice not only strengthened his body but also deepened his connection to his inner self.

Journaling became a way to reflect on his spiritual journey, capturing moments of insight and personal growth. Through writing, he documented his evolving perspectives and set intentions for living authentically.

As Rohan delved deeper into spirituality, he experienced a profound transformation within himself. He no longer sought validation from others or measured success by external standards. Instead, he found fulfilment in aligning his actions with his values and serving others with compassion.

Through his spiritual exploration, Rohan began to discern his life's purpose more clearly. He understood that every experience—whether joyful or challenging—was an opportunity for growth and learning. His interactions with others became infused with kindness and empathy, fostering deeper connections and meaningful relationships.

As weeks turned into months, Rohan's outlook on life began to shift. He felt more grounded, more connected to the world around him. The pressures and challenges were still there, but they no longer seemed insurmountable. He started talking to his parents about his feelings and sought support from a school counsellor.

One day, Rohan decided to visit an ISKCON temple his grandmother frequented. He remembered her stories about Lord Krishna and the peace she found in her spiritual practices. The temple was serene, filled with the sound of devotional songs and the scent of incense. He felt an unexpected sense of belonging.

Rohan started attending the temple regularly, participating in the kirtans and listening to the teachings of A.C. Bhakti Vedanta Swami Prabhupada. The principles of Bhakti Yoga—devotion, compassion, and selflessness—resonated with him deeply. He found solace in the community, and for the first time in a long time, he felt a sense of purpose.

Through spirituality, Rohan discovered the strength within himself to face his challenges. He learned to let go of the need for external validation and embraced the journey of self-discovery and inner peace. His grades improved, but more importantly, he rediscovered joy and meaning in his life.

Rohan's transformation didn't go unnoticed. His friends and family saw the positive change and began asking him about his journey. Inspired by his experience, Rohan started a mindfulness and meditation club at school, sharing the tools that had helped him overcome his struggles.

He became a beacon of hope for others, showing that no matter how dark things might seem, there is always a way out. Through spirituality, Rohan not only healed himself but also inspired others to find their own paths to inner peace and resilience.

Rohan's journey was far from over. Life would continue to present challenges, but he now had the tools to navigate them. With spirituality as his guiding light, he embraced the future with hope and confidence, ready to face whatever came his way.

And so, Rohan's story became a testament to the transformative power of spirituality, a reminder that even in our darkest moments, there is always a way to find light and purpose.

The Student's World

High school, especially teenage is a world unto itself, filled with challenges, triumphs, and growth opportunities. It's a time when students like you are trying to figure out who you are, what you want, and how to navigate the often confusing and overwhelming landscape of academics, social life, and personal development. This chapter dives into the unique world of students, exploring the pressures, the joys, and the potential for spiritual growth that lies within this transformative period.

Let's break down this world into some key areas that impact your lives the most.

1. The Academic Pressure Cooker

Alright, let's talk about schoolwork. You know how it feels like you're constantly buried under a mountain of homework, projects, and exams? It's like being in a pressure cooker that never seems to let up. The expectations are sky-high—from your parents, your teachers, and sometimes, even from yourself.

Her I am remembering Muskan, one of my brightest children of class 12. She's the class topper, always on top of her game, juggling a dozen activities while maintaining perfect grades. Sounds impressive, right? But what you don't see are the sleepless nights, the anxiety attacks, and the constant fear of failure she hides behind her smile. Ananya's story isn't unique; it's the reality for many students today.

Why This Happens:
- The competition is fierce. Everyone wants to get into the best colleges, win scholarships, and land amazing jobs.
- There's this constant comparison with peers. If someone scores higher, it feels like you've fallen behind.
- Parents and teachers often have high expectations, sometimes forgetting that everyone has their limits.

2. Social Media and Self-Expectation

Let's be real—social media is a huge part of our lives. It's where we connect, share, and sometimes, compare ourselves to others. Ever felt like your life is boring because you're not vacationing in Bali, acing every test, or hanging out with a squad that looks straight out of a TV show? Yeah, me too.

I remember Piyush, one of my most sweet student, a regular teenager who loves scrolling through Instagram. He sees his friends posting about their fantastic lives and begins to doubt his own worth. He starts to think, "Why am I not as cool or successful as them?" This comparison trap is a major source of stress and insecurity.

Why This Happens:
- Social media often showcases the highlights of people's lives, not the full story. It's easy to forget that everyone has their struggles.

- The number of likes, comments, and followers can make you feel validated—or not. It's like a popularity contest that never ends.

- The pressure to maintain a perfect online persona can be exhausting and lead to a lot of stress.

3. The Wrong Definition of Being Cool

Now, let's talk about the idea of being "cool." What does it even mean? Is it about wearing the latest trends, being popular, or doing things just to fit in? Sometimes, the pressure to be cool can lead you down paths that aren't true to who you really are.

Alright, let's get real about what's often mistaken for being "cool" these days. Ever hear the phrase "Bhai Ka Swag"? It's like a badge some people wear to show off their arrogance, thinking it makes them look tough or important. But here's the truth: being rude, using abusive language, and acting superior doesn't make you cool—it just makes you look insecure.

Take for example, the trend of posting pictures and videos on social media of bunking classes, smoking hookah, or drinking alcohol at a young age. Teenagers do it to seem rebellious and edgy, but honestly, it's just dangerous and irresponsible. It might get some likes and comments, but it doesn't earn you real respect.

Think about how you feel when you see someone being admired for something superficial, like having the latest gadget or being able to pull off a daring prank. It's easy to get caught up in wanting to emulate that. But remember, being true to yourself is the real cool.

Why This Happens:
- Media and society often glorify certain behaviours and appearances, making them seem desirable.
- Peer pressure can make you feel like you need to conform to certain standards to be accepted.
- The desire to fit in and be liked is a natural part of growing up, but it can sometimes lead to compromising your values.

4. Fiddling with Relationships

Alright, let's talk about something that often gets messed up in the pursuit of being "cool": relationships. Dating just to impress others or to fit in with a certain group might seem like a good idea at first, but trust me, it's a recipe for disaster.

Imagine This: You start dating someone because your friends think it's cool or because you want to be known as a "stud." But deep down, you're not really into it or ready for it. You end up neglecting your studies, your goals, and worst of all, your own feelings.

Why This Happens:
- Peer pressure can make you feel like you need to have a partner to be accepted or popular.
- Social media and movies often glamorize relationships, making them seem like a must-have status symbol.
- It's easy to get caught up in the excitement of a new relationship without thinking about the long-term consequences.

5. Peer Pressure and Social Dynamics

Let's dive deeper into the world of peer pressure and social dynamics, because let's face it, it's a big deal in high school and beyond. Peer pressure isn't just about friends pushing you to do something you're not comfortable with—it's about the constant tug-of-war between fitting in and staying true to yourself.

Peer pressure is like a silent force that can influence your decisions, behaviours, and even your sense of identity. It's not always obvious; sometimes it's subtle comments, expectations, or even just seeing what everyone else is doing on social media. Whether it's about how you dress, who you hang out with, or what you do on weekends, peer pressure can make you feel like you have to conform to be accepted.

Think about Bhavna, a diligent student from a financially struggling family. Despite her potential, she felt pressured to fit in with her peers, who often flaunted their wealth and latest gadgets. This pressure made her feel inadequate and led her to question her own worth.

Why This Happens:

- **Fear of Missing Out (FOMO)-** You see your friends doing something fun or exciting, and you don't want to be left out.

- **Desire for Acceptance-** Everyone wants to feel liked and included. Sometimes, going along with the crowd seems like the easiest way to fit in.

- **Lack of Confidence-** It can be hard to stand up for what you believe in when everyone around you is doing something different.

Life as a student can be overwhelming, right? Between exams, social media, friendships, and expectations from parents and teachers, it sometimes feels like you're juggling a dozen balls in the air. But what if I told you that spirituality could be the missing piece to help you manage it all? Yep, spirituality isn't just for monks or your grandparents; it's for you too. Let's dive into why spirituality matters and how it can make a difference in your life.

1. Stress Management Superpowers

Let's talk about stress. We all know it; we all hate it. Whether it's exams, homework, or drama with friends, stress is a constant companion. Spirituality can help you manage it like a pro.

Imagine this scenario: You've got a massive exam coming up, and the pressure is on. Instead of freaking out, you take a few minutes to meditate or do some deep breathing. Suddenly, you're calmer, more focused, and ready to tackle that test. Spirituality offers tools like meditation, mindfulness, and deep breathing exercises that can help you relax and keep your cool. Think of it as your personal superhero kit for stress.

2. Mindfulness: Living in the Moment

Ever feel like your brain is running a million miles a minute? Between Instagram, TikTok, and Snapchat, it's hard to find a moment of peace. That's where mindfulness comes in. It's about being present in the moment and fully engaging with what you're doing.

When you practice mindfulness, you'll notice things you never paid attention to before. The way the sun feels on your face, the sound of birds chirping, or even the taste of your favourite snack. It's like turning up the volume on life! Plus, being mindful can help you focus better in class and improve your grades. Win-win, right?

3. Discovering Your True Self

Let's get a bit deep here. Do you ever feel like you're not really sure who you are or what you want? It's totally normal, especially with all the pressure to fit in and be "cool." Spirituality can help you connect with your true self and figure out what really matters to you.

Think of spirituality as a journey to discover the real you. It's not about fitting into a mold or doing what everyone else is doing. It's about understanding your values, your passions, and what makes you unique. When you connect with your true self, you'll feel more confident and less worried about what others think.

4. Building Compassion and Empathy

Let's face it, the world can be a tough place. People can be mean, and it's easy to get caught up in negativity. But spirituality teaches us the importance of compassion—both for ourselves and others.

When you practice compassion, you're kinder to yourself and those around you. You start to see things from other people's perspectives and understand their struggles. This can make your relationships stronger and create a more positive environment at school. Imagine a world where everyone looks out for each other—that's the power of compassion!

5. Making Sense of the Big Questions

Life is full of big questions. Why are we here? What's the purpose of life? What happens after we die? These questions can be confusing and even a bit scary. Spirituality doesn't necessarily provide all the answers, but it helps you explore these questions in a meaningful way.

When you delve into spirituality, you start to see life from a bigger perspective. You realize that there's more to life than grades, popularity, and social media likes. This can give you a sense of purpose and direction, helping you navigate the ups and downs of life with more grace and resilience.

6. Fun and Joy in the Journey

Here's the best part: spirituality isn't all serious and boring. It can be fun and bring a lot of joy into your life! Whether it's practicing yoga, going on nature walks, or simply spending quiet time reflecting, there are many ways to make spirituality enjoyable.

Remember, it's your journey. There's no right or wrong way to be spiritual. Find what works for you and what makes you happy. The goal is to feel more connected, peaceful, and joyful.

So, there you have it, friends. Spirituality isn't just for ancient gurus or people living in monasteries. It's for you—right here, right now. It's about finding inner peace, discovering your true self, and living a life filled with compassion and joy.

Give it a try. Start with small steps like meditating for a few minutes each day or practicing mindfulness when you're out and about. You might be surprised at how much better you feel. And remember, it's okay to ask for guidance. Talk to a teacher, a parent, or a friend who practices spirituality. They'll be happy to help you on your journey.

Embrace spirituality and watch how it transforms your life. You've got this!

The Path Unseen
"A Tale of Friendship and Spiritual Awakening"

Chapter - 1
The Bold Spirit

Neha was the kind of girl who could brighten any room just by walking into it. Her laughter was infectious, and her energy seemed boundless. Whether she was debating fiercely in the school auditorium or rallying classmates for a charity drive, she always seemed to be in the midst of something exciting.

During one of the school's cultural fests, she was at the centre of a group of friends, animatedly discussing plans for an upcoming event.

"Hey, have you guys heard about the talent show next month?" Neha exclaimed, her eyes sparkling with enthusiasm.

"Yeah, I heard! Are you planning to perform?" one of her friends asked, leaning in with interest.

Neha flashed a mischievous grin. "Of course! You know me, always up for a bit of drama," she replied, eliciting laughter from the group.

Her confidence and humour were magnetic. Even in casual conversations, Neha's presence was undeniable. She had a way of drawing people in with her witty remarks and genuine interest in everyone around her.

As the day progressed, Neha effortlessly connected with everyone, from freshmen to seniors. She seemed to know everyone's name and had a knack for making everyone feel included. It was clear that she thrived on the energy of social interactions and the thrill of new experiences.

Later, during a break in the festivities, Neha was chatting with a teacher near the refreshment stall.

"Hi there! Enjoying the fest?" the teacher asked, striking up a conversation.

Neha turned with a bright smile. "Oh, absolutely! These events are my favourite. It's like a chance to bring the whole school together, you know?"

The teacher nodded, impressed by her enthusiasm. "You seem to be everywhere, Neha. How do you manage to juggle so much?"

She chuckled, her eyes crinkling at the corners. "Oh, you know, just trying to make the most of high school. It's all about balancing academics with a bit of fun, right?"

Her casual confidence intrigued the teacher. Here was someone who not only embraced school life but also seemed to thrive in it.

At home, Neha's family dinners were lively affairs filled with laughter and animated discussions. Her parents admired her outgoing nature and encouraged her to pursue her passions wholeheartedly.

"So, Neha, how was school today?" her father asked one evening, sipping tea at the dinner table.

Neha grinned. "Great, Dad! We're planning this amazing charity event next month. I can't wait to get started."

Her mother chimed in, "That's wonderful, dear. But don't forget to keep up with your studies too."

Neha nodded enthusiastically. "Of course, Mom! I've got everything under control."

Her family admired her drive and zest for life, but little did they know that beneath Neha's confident facade, there were struggles and challenges waiting to unfold, shaping her journey in unexpected ways.

Her confidence was infectious, and her free-spirited nature drew others to her like moths to a flame. Neha had a way of making even the most mundane tasks seem exciting, whether it was studying for exams or planning the annual school play. She had a sharp wit and a quick tongue, never afraid to speak her mind or challenge the status quo. This boldness earned her both admirers and detractors, but Neha took it all in stride, never letting anyone dull her sparkle.

Despite her outgoing persona, Neha had a sensitive side too. She cared deeply about her friends and would go out of her way to help anyone in need. Her empathy and kindness were as remarkable as her charisma, making her someone everyone wanted to be around.

Chapter - 2
Echoes of Solitude

The school's annual debate competition was a highly anticipated event, showcasing the best orators and critical thinkers among the students. Neha and Riya, close friends since middle school, had always supported each other's academic pursuits. They often practiced together and shared study notes, fostering a bond built on mutual respect and encouragement.

On the day of the debate competition, tensions ran high as students gathered in the auditorium, eager to display their debating skills. Neha and Riya both made it to the final round, a testament to their dedication and intellect. As they stood on opposite sides of the podium, the atmosphere crackled with anticipation.

Neha eloquently presented her arguments, capturing the audience's attention with her persuasive delivery and logical reasoning. Her confidence and poise earned her praise from the judges and admiration from her peers. Riya, on the other hand, struggled to match Neha's charisma, stumbling over her words and appearing less composed under pressure.

As the competition progressed, a seed of jealousy took root in Riya's mind. She had always prided herself on her academic achievements, and seeing Neha shine so brightly stirred up conflicting emotions. In a fleeting moment of insecurity, Riya began to perceive Neha's success as a threat rather than a celebration of their shared accomplishments.

Later that evening, as they gathered with their friends for a post-competition celebration, the atmosphere subtly shifted. Conversations buzzed around the results, with Neha's impressive performance becoming a topic of admiration. Riya's unease grew as she overheard whispers among their friends, some marvelling at Neha's confidence while others subtly questioned Riya's own abilities.

Unable to contain her feelings any longer, Riya's emotions spilled over in a private conversation with Anushka, another close friend in their circle.

"I just feel like Neha always has to be the centre of attention," Riya confided, her voice tinged with frustration. "She acts like she's better than everyone else."

Anushka, trying to calm the situation, replied cautiously, "I think you're reading too much into it, Riya. Neha was just doing her best, like always."

But Riya was unconvinced. The seed of jealousy had taken root, fuelling her perception of Neha's actions as self-centred and arrogant. Misinterpretations of Neha's enthusiasm and confidence began to spread among their friends, slowly eroding the trust and camaraderie that had once defined their group.

Over the following days, whispers and subtle gestures began to distance Neha from her friends. Small misunderstandings grew into rumours, painting Neha in a negative light. Some friends began to avoid her, while others treated her with cautious politeness, unsure of how to navigate the tension that had emerged.

Neha, unaware of the brewing discord, continued to approach her friendships with the same openness and enthusiasm. She noticed the subtle shifts in her friends' behaviour but attributed it to the stress of upcoming exams and personal challenges. It wasn't until Anushka finally confronted her with the rumours that Neha realized the extent of the rift that had formed.

"Neha, there's been talk," Anushka started tentatively, choosing her words carefully. "Some people think you were trying to overshadow Riya during the debate. They're saying you're too competitive."

Neha's heart sank as she processed Anushka's words. She had never intended to undermine Riya or make anyone feel inferior. The realization that her friends had misunderstood her intentions hit her hard, shaking the foundation of trust and support she had taken for granted.

As Neha tried to explain herself, the rift deepened. Her attempts to clarify only seemed to fuel the gossip and speculation among their friends. Hurt and bewildered, Neha withdrew into herself, grappling with feelings of betrayal and confusion.

As rumours and misunderstandings continued to swirl around Neha, the once vibrant school corridors began to feel alien and cold. What had initially been a close-knit circle of friends now seemed distant and guarded.

Neha noticed the subtle shifts in her friends' behaviour—sidelong glances, hushed conversations that fell silent when she approached, and invitations that never came. At first, she dismissed it as the stress of exams or personal issues affecting her friends. But as days turned into weeks, the pattern became undeniable.

One afternoon, Neha found herself walking alone down the corridor, her footsteps echoing in the emptiness. She spotted Riya and Anushka chatting animatedly with a group of their classmates near the notice board. Normally, she would have joined them without hesitation, but today she hesitated.

Taking a deep breath to steady herself, Neha approached the group. "Hey, what's up?" she asked, trying to sound casual.

Riya glanced at Anushka, then back at Neha, her expression guarded. "Oh, hey Neha," she replied, her tone lacking its usual warmth.

Anushka shifted uncomfortably, avoiding Neha's gaze. "Um, we were just discussing the upcoming history project," she offered lamely.

Neha felt a knot form in her stomach. She could sense the distance between them, a palpable barrier that had grown in the wake of the rumours and misunderstandings. "Is everything okay?" she asked, her voice tinged with concern.

Riya hesitated, exchanging a quick glance with Anushka before responding carefully, "Yeah, everything's fine. Just busy with school stuff, you know."

Despite their reassurances, Neha couldn't shake the feeling of being excluded, of standing on the outside looking in. The once effortless camaraderie now felt strained, each interaction tinged with an unspoken tension.

Over the next few days, Neha's attempts to bridge the gap only seemed to exacerbate the situation. She tried reaching out to her friends individually, inviting them for study sessions or lunch outings, but the responses were lukewarm at best. Some made excuses, citing other commitments or simply brushed off her invitations with vague promises to catch up later.

Frustration and hurt gnawed at Neha's spirit. She couldn't understand why her friends had turned away from her so suddenly. Had she truly done something wrong? Or was it simply a case of misunderstanding blown out of proportion?

One afternoon, Neha finally confronted Riya and Anushka after school, her frustration boiling over. "Can we talk?" she asked, her voice tinged with a mix of anger and hurt.

Riya exchanged a hesitant glance with Anushka before nodding reluctantly. "Sure, Neha. What's on your mind?"

Taking a deep breath to steady herself, Neha launched into her feelings. "I feel like you guys have been avoiding me," she began, her voice trembling slightly. "Ever since the debate competition, things have been different. I don't understand what's changed."

Anushka looked uncomfortable, shifting on her feet. "Neha, it's not that simple," she started, her words careful. "There have been rumours—about you being too competitive, trying to overshadow others. It's been causing tension among our friends."

Anushka's voice carried a hint of hesitation, reflecting the delicate nature of the conversation. She glanced at Riya, who nodded subtly, prompting her to continue.

"It's not just the rumours," Anushka continued, her gaze returning to Neha with a mix of sympathy and unease. "Some people feel like you're always trying to prove yourself, like you think you're better than everyone else."

Neha felt a knot form in her stomach, her disbelief palpable. "But that's not true," she interjected, her voice tinged with frustration. "I never meant to make anyone feel that way. I just want to do my best."

Riya sighed softly; her expression troubled. "Neha, it's about perception," she explained gently. "People see what they want to see. And right now, the perception is that you're pushing too hard, that you think you're the best."

Neha's mind raced, trying to reconcile the image her friends were describing with her own intentions. She had always believed in giving her all, in striving for excellence, but now she realized how it might have been misunderstood. The realization stung—she had unwittingly alienated her friends by simply being herself, by pursuing her passions with Vigour.

"I didn't mean to come across that way," Neha murmured, her voice betraying a mix of hurt and confusion. "I just want us to do well as a team."

Anushka nodded sympathetically, her discomfort evident. "We know, Neha," she said softly. "But sometimes, it's not just about what we intend. It's about how others perceive our actions."

The conversation left Neha feeling vulnerable and exposed. She had always prided herself on her honesty and openness, but now she felt misunderstood and unfairly judged, she saw how it had inadvertently caused rifts among her friends. The weight of their perceptions hung heavy on her shoulders, challenging her to rethink how she approached her relationships and her ambitions.

In the days that followed, Neha found herself retreating further into solitude. The once bustling school corridors now felt empty and indifferent. Lunch breaks were spent alone in the library, studying or lost in her thoughts. The laughter and camaraderie she had once enjoyed with her friends seemed like a distant memory.

As Neha navigated this newfound isolation, she grappled with a mix of emotions—hurt, anger, and a profound sense of loneliness. She couldn't shake the feeling of being judged and cast aside, unsure of how to mend the fractured relationships or regain the trust she had lost.

With her social life in turmoil, Neha found herself increasingly adrift in a sea of confusion and self-doubt. Once driven and focused on her studies and extracurricular activities, she now struggled to concentrate. The whispers of rumours and the strain in her friendships had taken a toll on her mental well-being, casting a shadow over everything she once excelled in.

In class, Neha's teachers noticed a marked decline in her academic performance. Her once vibrant participation dwindled, replaced by a withdrawn demeanour and distracted gaze. Assignments, which she once tackled with enthusiasm, now seemed daunting and insurmountable.

Ms. Sharma, her English teacher, noticed the change first. During a discussion on poetry analysis, Neha, who used to eagerly contribute, now sat silent, her eyes distant. After class one day, Ms. Sharma gently approached Neha.

"Is everything alright, Neha?" Ms. Sharma asked, her tone laced with concern.

Neha looked up, startled. She hadn't realized she was being noticed. "Um, yeah, I'm fine," she replied vaguely, avoiding Ms. Sharma's gaze.

Ms. Sharma paused, studying Neha with a perceptive eye. "Your grades have been slipping lately," she ventured cautiously. "Is there something going on that's bothering you?"

Neha hesitated, torn between wanting to confide and the fear of being judged or misunderstood again. Finally, she sighed, feeling a surge of frustration and helplessness. "It's just... everything," she admitted quietly. "Things have been rough lately."

Ms. Sharma nodded understandingly, her expression kind. "If you ever want to talk, I'm here for you," she offered sincerely. "Sometimes it helps to share what's on your mind."

Neha managed a small smile, touched by Ms. Sharma's genuine concern. "Thanks, Ms. Sharma," she murmured gratefully.

As the weeks passed, Neha's grades continued to slip. Her once meticulous notes became haphazard, and her essays lacked the depth and clarity they once had. The harder she tried to focus, the more her mind wandered to the fractured friendships and the lingering doubts about herself.

During a parent-teacher meeting, Neha's parents expressed concern over her sudden decline in grades. Mr. and Mrs. Verma, who had always supported Neha's ambitions, were now at a loss for how to help their daughter.

"She's always been so driven," Mrs. Verma said with a worried frown. "I don't understand why she's suddenly struggling."

Ms. Sharma, who had requested the meeting to discuss Neha's academic performance, leaned forward sympathetically. "It's not uncommon for students to face challenges, especially when there are other things weighing on their minds," she explained gently. "Neha has a lot of potential, but I think she's struggling with some personal issues right now."

Mr. Verma nodded thoughtfully. "Is there anything we can do to help her?" he asked earnestly.

Ms. Sharma smiled reassuringly. "Just be there for her," she advised. "Encourage her to talk about what's bothering her, and let her know that she's not alone."

The conversation weighed heavily on Neha's mind as she navigated through her days, feeling increasingly isolated and adrift. She knew she needed to reach out, to find a way to untangle the knots of confusion and reclaim her focus. But the fear of judgment and the uncertainty of how to bridge the gaps loomed large, leaving her trapped in a cycle of academic struggle and emotional turmoil.

Chapter - 3
Revival

Amidst her isolation, Neha found herself wandering aimlessly during the sports period on the school's expansive field. The usual chatter and laughter of her peers felt distant as she walked alone, lost in her thoughts.

Under the shade of an ancient banyan tree, Neha noticed Priyanshi, a senior known for her calm demeanour and thoughtful presence. Priyanshi was sitting quietly, flipping through a book that Neha recognized as a collection of spiritual teachings.

Curious, Neha approached cautiously. "Hi, Priyanshi Didi," she greeted, her voice tinged with a mix of curiosity and vulnerability.

Priyanshi looked up, her serene eyes meeting Neha's troubled gaze. "Hello, Neha," she replied warmly, closing her book and gesturing for Neha to sit beside her.

Neha hesitated for a moment before settling down on the grass next to Priyanshi. "You always seem so calm and composed," she admitted, her voice tinged with admiration and a hint of longing.

Priyanshi smiled gently. "Appearances can be deceiving," she said softly. "We all have our struggles and challenges."

Neha nodded, feeling a sense of relief in Priyanshi's honesty. "I've been feeling so lost lately," she confessed, her voice barely above a whisper. "Everything seems to be falling apart."

Priyanshi listened attentively, her presence offering a comforting reassurance. "Sometimes, when we feel lost, it helps to reconnect with ourselves," she suggested gently.

Neha looked at Priyanshi, intrigued by her words. "How do you mean?"

Priyanshi paused thoughtfully before replying. "Have you ever explored spirituality as a way to find inner peace and clarity?" she asked, her voice soft yet confident.

Neha shook her head slightly. "Not really," she admitted. "I've heard about it, but I never really understood how it could help."

Priyanshi nodded understandingly. "Spirituality isn't just about rituals or beliefs," she explained. "It's about understanding ourselves better, finding meaning in our experiences, and learning to navigate through life's challenges with grace."

Neha listened intently, feeling a sense of curiosity and hope stirring within her. "But how do you start?" she wondered aloud.

Priyanshi smiled warmly. "It starts with self-reflection and exploring what resonates with you," she suggested. "For me, reading and reflecting on spiritual teachings has been a source of guidance and strength."

As they talked, Neha found herself opening up more and more to Priyanshi. She shared her struggles with friendships, the misunderstandings that had led to her isolation, and the impact it had on her academics and personal life.

Priyanshi listened attentively, offering insights and gentle encouragement along the way. "It's okay to feel lost sometimes," she reassured Neha. "What matters is how we choose to respond and grow from those experiences."

Their conversation continued for hours, flowing seamlessly from one topic to another. Priyanshi, sensing Neha's readiness, gently introduced the teachings of the Bhagavad Gita into their discussion.

"Neha, have you ever heard of the Bhagavad Gita?" Priyanshi asked, her voice filled with reverence for the ancient text.

Neha shook her head, intrigued by the mention of something new. "No, not really. What is it about?"

Priyanshi opened her book to a marked page and began to explain. "The Bhagavad Gita is a profound spiritual scripture that offers insights into life's dilemmas and challenges," she explained. "It teaches us about duty, righteousness, and the path to inner peace."

Neha listened attentively as Priyanshi shared a verse that resonated deeply with her current struggles.

उद्धरेदात्मनात्मानं नात्मानमवसादयेत् ।
आत्मैव ह्यात्मनो बन्धुरात्मैव रिपुरात्मनः ॥

"Elevate yourself through the power of your mind, and not degrade yourself, for the mind can be the friend and also the enemy of the self."

"Here, Neha," Priyanshi said, pointing to a passage. " This verse emphasizes the importance of self-control and introspection. It teaches that one should uplift oneself through one's own mind and not degrade oneself, as the mind can either be a friend or an enemy depending on how it is used. "

Neha read the verse silently, feeling a sense of clarity wash over her. The teachings seemed to speak directly to her current situation, offering a perspective that she had not considered before.

"Wow," Neha breathed, looking up at Priyanshi with newfound admiration. "I never thought spirituality could be so practical and insightful."

Priyanshi smiled warmly. "Spirituality is a journey of self-discovery and growth," she said. "It helps us understand ourselves and the world around us with compassion and clarity."

From that day forward, Neha embarked on a journey of exploring spirituality guided by Priyanshi's wisdom. The teachings of the Bhagavad Gita became a guiding light, helping Neha navigate through her challenges with newfound strength and resilience.

Intrigued by Priyanshi's calm demeanor and wise counsel, Neha began meeting her regularly. Priyanshi sensed Neha's turmoil and gently introduced her to spiritual practices that gradually became an anchor amidst the storm of emotions.

Their meetings often took place in a quiet corner of the school garden during lunch breaks. Priyanshi started by teaching Neha the basics of meditation, guiding her through calming breathing exercises and techniques to quiet the mind. Initially skeptical, Neha found herself gradually relaxing into the practice, finding moments of peace she hadn't experienced in a long time.

"Neha, meditation is about connecting with your inner self," Priyanshi explained one afternoon as they sat under the shade of a banyan tree. "It helps us to quiet the noise around us and within us, allowing us to listen to our true thoughts and feelings."

As Neha began to embrace meditation, Priyanshi introduced her to readings from the Bhagavad Gita, a spiritual classic that offered profound insights into life's challenges and the path to inner peace. One particular verse resonated deeply with Neha:

"Perform your obligatory duty, because action is indeed better than inaction. Even the maintenance of your body would not be possible through inaction." (Bhagavad Gita 3.8)

"This verse teaches us the importance of taking action, not for the results, but because it's our duty," Priyanshi explained, pointing to the passage in Neha's book. "It's about focusing on doing what's right and letting go of attachment to the outcome."

Neha found herself reflecting on this teaching throughout the day, applying it to her interactions with others and her academic pursuits. She realized that by focusing on the process rather than the outcome, she could alleviate some of the pressure she felt from societal expectations and personal goals.

In addition to the Bhagavad Gita, Priyanshi shared teachings from Swami Vivekananda, emphasizing self-confidence, self-reliance, and the importance of seeking truth within oneself. Neha found solace in these teachings, which encouraged her to trust her instincts and develop a deeper understanding of her own values and beliefs.

Through meditation, introspection, and the study of spiritual texts, Neha embarked on a journey of self-discovery and personal growth. The chaos and uncertainty that had once clouded her mind began to dissipate, replaced by a sense of clarity and purpose.

As Neha continued to meet with Priyanshi and delve deeper into spirituality, she found herself more grounded, resilient, and at peace with herself and the world around her. The journey had just begun, but Neha knew she was on the path to finding inner strength and fulfilment.

As Neha delved deeper into spirituality, she started to see her past actions and reactions from a different perspective. She realized her own role in the misunderstandings with her friends and began to forgive herself and others. With Aarav's guidance, she learned to channel her boldness into compassion and understanding.

Armed with newfound wisdom, Neha reached out to her friends with humility and honesty. Some were skeptical at first, but Neha's genuine efforts to mend relationships gradually won them over. She apologized for her part in the misunderstandings and expressed her desire to rebuild trust.

Slowly, Neha found herself surrounded by friends again. The school corridors echoed with laughter and chatter once more. Her academic performance improved as she regained focus and confidence. Neha continued her spiritual journey, now understanding that true strength lay not just in boldness, but in empathy and inner peace.

Practices for Spiritual Growth

Hey there, young minds! Now that you've journeyed through the previous chapters and have a grasp on what spirituality is and the profound impact it can have on your life, let's dive deeper. Today, we're going to explore practical spiritual practices that can truly enhance your well-being and personal growth. These aren't about rituals or something out of a fantasy movie; instead, they are real, practical tools you can use in your everyday life to find balance, purpose, and peace. Let's get started!

Why Spiritual Growth Matters

First things first, what exactly is spiritual growth, and why should you care about it? Well, think of it as nurturing your inner self—the part of you that thinks, feels, and wonders about the bigger picture of life. In our fast-paced world of studies, friendships, and social media, it's easy to get caught up in the noise and forget to listen to our own thoughts and feelings.

Spiritual growth helps you connect with what really matters to you beyond the surface of daily routines. It's about finding inner peace, understanding yourself better, and feeling connected to something greater than yourself—whether that's nature, humanity, or a higher power you believe in.

Let's see how some of the young and famous personalities of the modern age view and integrate spiritual growth into their lives, and why it matters to them:

1) **Eckhart Tolle:** A renowned spiritual teacher and author known for his teachings on mindfulness, presence, and living in the moment. His books like "The Power of Now" and "A New Earth" have inspired millions worldwide to find inner peace and spiritual awakening.

2) **Jay Shetty:** Former monk turned motivational speaker and author; Jay Shetty blends ancient wisdom with modern-day practicality. He's known for his insightful videos and books that help people navigate life's challenges through mindfulness, meditation, and personal growth.

3) **Ranveer Allahbadia (BeerBiceps):** A popular Indian YouTuber and fitness enthusiast, Ranveer Allahbadia promotes holistic well-being, including mental health and positivity. He shares practical tips on fitness, nutrition, and personal development to inspire young audiences.

4) **Amogh Lila Das:** A spiritual teacher and speaker who interprets ancient Vedic wisdom, particularly teachings from the Bhagavad Gita, in a modern context. He focuses on spiritual growth, mindfulness, and applying timeless principles to contemporary life.

5) **Dalai Lama:** The spiritual leader of Tibetan Buddhism and a global advocate for peace, compassion, and interfaith dialogue. His teachings on kindness, empathy, and inner peace have touched millions and earned him the Nobel Peace Prize.

6) **Thich Nhat Hanh:** A Vietnamese Buddhist monk, peace activist, and author known for his teachings on mindfulness, peace, and social justice. His books like "The Miracle of Mindfulness" have made Buddhist practices accessible and relevant to a global audience.

7) **Deepak Chopra:** A pioneer in integrative medicine and personal transformation, Deepak Chopra combines Eastern spiritual teachings with Western science. He's authored numerous bestsellers on mind-body healing, meditation, and spiritual wellness.

8) **Shivani Didi (Brahma Kumari Shivani):** A spiritual teacher and motivational speaker associated with the Brahma Kumari's organization. She focuses on meditation, positive thinking, and personal transformation to help individuals lead fulfilling lives.

9) **Jaya Kishori:** A popular young spiritual orator and singer known for her discourses on spirituality, devotion (bhakti), and moral values. She travels extensively, delivering motivational talks and bhajans that inspire audiences across India.

10) **Vivek Bindra:** A motivational speaker, leadership trainer, and founder of Bada Business. He incorporates spiritual principles into his teachings on business and personal development, helping people achieve success while maintaining inner peace and balance.

11) **Kumar Vishwas:** A poet and motivational speaker known for his inspiring orations. He often integrates themes of spirituality, personal growth, and resilience into his poetry and speeches, resonating deeply with young audiences.

These personalities come from diverse backgrounds and traditions, but they share a common goal of promoting spiritual growth, mindfulness, and personal development among their audiences. Their teachings resonate with people seeking inner peace, clarity, and a deeper understanding of life's purpose.

Spiritual growth matters profoundly because it addresses the core of human existence beyond material pursuits, focusing on inner peace, purpose, and fulfilment. Here are some detailed reasons with real-life examples:

1) **Inner Peace and Emotional Resilience:** Spiritual growth often involves practices like meditation, mindfulness, and prayer, which help individuals cultivate inner peace and emotional resilience. For instance, Eckhart Tolle's teachings on mindfulness have helped many people manage stress and anxiety by staying present in the moment, rather than dwelling on past regrets or future worries.

2) **Clarity of Purpose:** Spiritual growth encourages individuals to reflect on their values and life goals. Jay Shetty, through his motivational talks and books, guides people to align their actions with their deeper purpose. For example, his own journey from a corporate career to becoming a monk illustrates how

spiritual introspection can lead to a more fulfilling life aligned with one's true calling.

3) **Compassion and Empathy:** Many spiritual teachings emphasize compassion and empathy towards others, fostering a sense of interconnectedness and community. The Dalai Lama exemplifies this through his advocacy for peace and non-violence, promoting dialogue and understanding among people from different backgrounds.

4) **Overcoming Adversity:** Spiritual growth provides a framework for finding meaning in adversity. Amogh Lila Das, drawing from the Bhagavad Gita, teaches how spiritual resilience can help individuals navigate life's challenges with grace and wisdom. His teachings resonate with those seeking guidance on resilience amidst personal struggles.

5) **Health and Well-being:** Studies have shown that spiritual practices contribute to improved mental health and overall well-being. Deepak Chopra integrates spiritual principles with modern medicine to promote holistic health, emphasizing the mind-body connection. His work illustrates how spiritual growth can enhance physical health and longevity.

6) **Personal Transformation:** Spiritual growth often involves a journey of personal transformation, where individuals evolve spiritually and morally. Shivani Didi's teachings on meditation and positive thinking inspire personal growth, empowering individuals to overcome negativity and cultivate a more compassionate outlook.

7) Legacy of Wisdom: Spiritual leaders like Thich Nhat Hanh have left a lasting legacy of wisdom through their teachings on mindfulness and peace. His example of living mindfully and advocating for social justice inspires people globally to embrace mindfulness as a path to individual and collective healing.

Now that you have understood the importance of spiritual growth and how it can change lives, let's explore four key practices that can help you on your journey. These practices are not about forcing beliefs or adding more tasks to your busy schedule. Instead, they're simple ways to bring more mindfulness, gratitude, and reflection into your life.

1) Mindfulness and Meditation Let's start with mindfulness and meditation. Have you ever felt overwhelmed by schoolwork, exams, or even social pressures? Mindfulness is all about being present in the moment, noticing your thoughts without judgment, and learning to focus your mind. Meditation, on the other hand, helps calm your thoughts and relax your body. Personalities like Eckhart Tolle, known for his teachings on mindfulness and presence, and Jay Shetty, a popular speaker on meditation and mindfulness, have shown how these practices can transform lives.

2) Gratitude and Journaling Next up, gratitude and journaling. Ever noticed how good it feels when someone says "thank you" for something you've done? Gratitude is like that, but for yourself. Keeping a gratitude journal—where you jot down things, you're thankful for each day—can shift your focus from what's going wrong to what's going right in your life. Personalities like Ranveer Allahbadia, known for promoting positivity and self-improvement through his YouTube channel, emphasize the power of gratitude in daily life.

3) Nature and Solitude Now, let's step outside into nature. Whether it's a park, a garden, or simply a quiet spot under a tree, spending time in nature can calm your mind and lift your spirits. It's a chance to disconnect from screens and connect with the beauty around you. Personalities like Amogh Lila Das, who shares spiritual wisdom and practices from the Bhagavad Gita and other texts, often highlight the healing power of nature and solitude.

4) Faith in God Lastly, faith in God—or whatever higher power you believe in. For many people, faith provides a sense of purpose, comfort during tough times, and a deeper connection with spiritual teachings. Whether you attend religious services, read scriptures, or simply reflect on your beliefs, nurturing faith can offer strength and guidance in your life's journey. Many spiritual leaders, like Dalai Lama, Thich Nhat Hanh, and Deepak Chopra, have inspired millions with their teachings on faith and spirituality.

These practices are tools you can use to find balance, peace, and a deeper understanding of yourself and the world around you. By integrating mindfulness, gratitude, nature, and faith into your daily routine, you can cultivate a more fulfilling and spiritually enriched life.

Mindfulness and Meditation

What is Mindfulness?
Mindfulness is the practice of being fully present and engaged in the current moment, aware of your thoughts, feelings, and surroundings without judgment. It's about living in the now rather than dwelling on the past or worrying about the future. Mindfulness helps you to observe your thoughts and feelings from a distance, without labelling them as good or bad.

What is Meditation?
Meditation is a technique used to develop mindfulness, often involving focused attention and controlled breathing. It's a mental exercise that involves relaxation, focus, and awareness. Meditation helps calm the mind, reduce stress, and improve concentration.

How to Practice Mindfulness and Meditation
1) **Find a Quiet Place:** Choose a quiet, comfortable place where you won't be disturbed. This could be a quiet room, a garden, or even a park bench.

2) **Get Comfortable:** Sit in a comfortable position with your back straight but not rigid. You can sit on a chair, a cushion, or directly on the floor. The key is to feel relaxed but alert.

3) **Focus on Your Breath:** Close your eyes and take a few deep breaths. Inhale slowly through your nose,

hold for a few seconds, and then exhale through your mouth. Pay attention to the sensation of the breath entering and leaving your body.

4) **Notice Your Thoughts:** As you focus on your breath, you'll notice your mind wandering. This is normal. Instead of trying to stop your thoughts, simply acknowledge them without judgment and gently bring your focus back to your breath.

5) **Start with Short Sessions:** Begin with just a few minutes each day and gradually increase the time as you become more comfortable with the practice. Even five minutes of meditation can make a significant difference.

6) **Use Guided Meditations:** If you're new to meditation, guided meditations can be very helpful. There are many apps and online resources with guided sessions that can help you get started.

Impact of Mindfulness and Meditation

1) **Reduces Stress:** Regular mindfulness and meditation practices can significantly reduce stress levels. By focusing on the present moment, you can let go of worries and anxieties about the past or future.

2) **Improves Concentration:** Meditation enhances your ability to concentrate and focus on tasks, which can improve your performance in school and other activities.

3) **Enhances Emotional Health:** Mindfulness helps you become more aware of your emotions and how to

manage them. It promotes emotional stability and reduces symptoms of anxiety and depression.

4) **Promotes Self-Awareness:** By observing your thoughts and feelings, you gain a deeper understanding of yourself, your habits, and your reactions. This self-awareness can lead to personal growth and better decision-making.

5) **Improves Physical Health:** Mindfulness and meditation can lower blood pressure, improve sleep, and boost the immune system. The relaxation response induced by meditation helps the body to repair and heal itself.

How to Integrate Mindfulness and Meditation into Your Daily Life

1) **Morning Routine:** Start your day with a few minutes of mindfulness or meditation. This sets a positive tone for the day and helps you stay focused and calm.

2) **Mindful Eating:** Pay attention to the taste, texture, and smell of your food. Eating mindfully can enhance your enjoyment of food and help with digestion.

3) **Mindful Walking:** When walking, focus on the sensation of your feet touching the ground and the rhythm of your steps. This can be a simple yet powerful way to practice mindfulness.

4) **Mindful Listening:** When talking to someone, give them your full attention. Listen to their words, observe their body language, and be fully present in the conversation.

5) Evening Routine: End your day with a short meditation session to unwind and reflect on the day. This can help you release any tension and prepare for a restful sleep.

Real-Life Examples of the Benefits of Mindfulness and Meditation

- **Eckhart Tolle:** The author of "The Power of Now" attributes his personal transformation and inner peace to the practice of mindfulness. His teachings emphasize the importance of living in the present moment.

- **Jay Shetty:** A former monk, Jay Shetty uses mindfulness and meditation to help people navigate life's challenges. He shares practical tips on how these practices can improve mental health and overall well-being.

- **Ranveer Allahbadia:** Known for promoting holistic well-being, Ranveer incorporates mindfulness and meditation into his fitness routines to enhance mental clarity and positivity.

In conclusion, mindfulness and meditation are powerful tools that can help you manage stress, improve concentration, and enhance your emotional well-being. By integrating these practices into your daily life, you can cultivate a sense of inner peace and balance that will benefit you in all areas of your life.

Gratitude and Journaling

What is Gratitude?
Gratitude is the practice of recognizing and appreciating the good things in your life. It's about focusing on what you have rather than what you lack. Expressing gratitude can lead to a more positive outlook on life and increase feelings of happiness and contentment.

What is Journaling?
Journaling is the act of writing down your thoughts, feelings, and experiences. It's a form of self-expression that can help you process emotions, reflect on your day, and gain insights into your life. Keeping a gratitude journal specifically involves recording things you are thankful for each day.

How to Practice Gratitude and Journaling
1) **Start a Gratitude Journal:** Get a notebook or use a digital app to create a gratitude journal. Each day, write down at least three things you are grateful for. These can be big things, like a supportive family, or small things, like a beautiful sunset.

2) **Be Specific:** When you write in your gratitude journal, be as specific as possible. Instead of writing "I'm grateful for my friends," write "I'm grateful for my friend Sarah who listened to me when I was feeling down today."

3) **Focus on the Positive:** Even on tough days, try to find something positive to be grateful for. It could be something as simple as having a warm bed to sleep in or a delicious meal.

4) **Reflect on Your Entries:** Periodically read back through your journal entries. This can help reinforce your feelings of gratitude and remind you of the good things in your life.

5) **Express Gratitude to Others:** Don't just keep your gratitude to yourself. Let others know when you appreciate them. A simple "thank you" can make a big difference in someone's day and strengthen your relationships.

6) **Include Affirmations:** Along with gratitude, you can write positive affirmations in your journal. These are statements that affirm your worth and abilities, such as "I am capable and strong" or "I deserve happiness."

Impact of Gratitude and Journaling

1) **Improves Mental Health:** Practicing gratitude has been shown to reduce symptoms of depression and anxiety. It shifts your focus from negative thoughts to positive ones, enhancing your overall mental well-being.

2) **Enhances Emotional Resilience:** Keeping a gratitude journal helps you develop a positive mindset, which can make you more resilient in the face of challenges. It trains your brain to look for the good in every situation.

3) **Strengthens Relationships:** Expressing gratitude to others can improve your relationships. It fosters a sense of connection and appreciation, making people feel valued and loved.

4) **Boosts Self-Esteem:** Journaling about positive experiences and affirmations can boost your self-esteem. It helps you recognize your achievements and the good qualities you possess.

5) **Reduces Stress:** Writing down what you're grateful for can reduce stress by shifting your focus away from worries and negative thoughts. It promotes a sense of calm and relaxation.

How to Integrate Gratitude and Journaling into Your Daily Life

1) **Morning Routine:** Start your day by writing down three things you are grateful for. This sets a positive tone for the day and helps you begin with a mindset of appreciation.

2) **End-of-Day Reflection:** Before going to bed, take a few minutes to reflect on your day and write down things you are thankful for. This can help you end the day on a positive note and prepare for a restful sleep.

3) **Gratitude Jar:** Keep a jar and some small pieces of paper in a place you see every day. Whenever you feel grateful, write it down and put it in the jar. At the end of the month or year, read through the notes to remind yourself of all the good things that happened.

4) **Gratitude Letters:** Write letters to people you are grateful for. You don't have to send them, but the act

of writing can help you focus on the positive aspects of your relationships.

5) **Gratitude Walk:** Take a walk and observe your surroundings. As you walk, think about the things you are grateful for. This combines the benefits of gratitude with physical activity and time spent in nature.

Real-Life Examples of the Benefits of Gratitude and Journaling

- **Ranveer Allahbadia (BeerBiceps):** Known for promoting positivity and self-improvement, Ranveer emphasizes the power of gratitude in daily life. He shares practical tips on how expressing gratitude can lead to a more fulfilling and happy life.

- **Jay Shetty:** Former monk and motivational speaker, Jay Shetty encourages people to practice gratitude and journaling to navigate life's challenges. He believes that these practices can transform one's outlook and improve mental health.

- **Jaya Kishori:** A young spiritual orator and singer, Jaya Kishori often speaks about the importance of gratitude in her discourses. She shares how being thankful can lead to a more peaceful and content life.

In conclusion, gratitude and journaling are simple yet powerful practices that can significantly enhance your mental and emotional well-being. By incorporating these habits into your daily routine, you can cultivate a more positive outlook, strengthen your relationships, and find joy in the little things.

Nature and Solitude

What is Nature and Solitude?
Nature: Connecting with nature involves spending time in natural settings like parks, forests, mountains, or even your backyard. It's about appreciating the beauty and tranquillity of the natural world, which can be a powerful antidote to the stress of modern life.

Solitude: Solitude means spending time alone, away from the hustle and bustle of daily activities. It's not about feeling lonely but rather about enjoying your own company, reflecting, and recharging your mental and emotional batteries.

How to Practice Nature and Solitude
1) **Take Regular Walks:** Make it a habit to take walks in nature. Whether it's a park, a trail, or just around your neighbourhood, walking outside can help you clear your mind and appreciate your surroundings.

2) **Create a Quiet Space:** Designate a spot in your home or garden where you can sit quietly and enjoy some alone time. This can be a place for meditation, reading, or simply being with your thoughts.

3) **Disconnect from Devices:** When spending time in nature or solitude, try to disconnect from your phone, tablet, or computer. This helps you fully engage with the present moment without distractions.

4) **Observe and Reflect:** While in nature, take time to observe the details around you—the sound of birds, the rustle of leaves, the feel of the breeze. Reflect on how these experiences make you feel and what they teach you about life.

5) **Practice Mindful Breathing:** Combine solitude with mindfulness by practicing deep breathing exercises. Sit quietly, close your eyes, and take slow, deep breaths, focusing on the rhythm of your breath and the sensations in your body.

6) **Journal in Nature:** Take your journal with you on nature outings. Writing down your thoughts and feelings while immersed in a natural setting can provide clarity and inspiration.

Impact of Nature and Solitude

1) **Reduces Stress:** Spending time in nature and solitude helps lower cortisol levels (the stress hormone) and can reduce feelings of anxiety and tension. It provides a peaceful escape from the demands of everyday life.

2) **Enhances Creativity:** Being in a natural environment and spending time alone can boost creativity. The quiet and beauty of nature stimulate the mind, allowing for new ideas and insights to flow.

3) **Improves Mental Health:** Regular exposure to nature and periods of solitude can improve mental health by reducing symptoms of depression and anxiety. It promotes a sense of calm and well-being.

4) **Boosts Physical Health:** Activities like walking, hiking, or gardening in natural settings are great for physical health. They encourage exercise, which benefits the heart, muscles, and overall fitness.

5) **Encourages Self-Reflection:** Solitude provides an opportunity for introspection. It allows you to think deeply about your life, your goals, and your values, helping you to understand yourself better and make more informed decisions.

How to Integrate Nature and Solitude into Your Daily Life

1) **Morning or Evening Walks:** Incorporate a walk into your daily routine, either in the morning to start your day or in the evening to unwind. This helps you connect with nature regularly.

2) **Weekend Nature Trips:** Plan short trips to natural spots like beaches, mountains, or nature reserves on weekends. These trips can provide a refreshing break from your routine and deepen your connection with nature.

3) **Gardening:** If you have space, start a garden. Gardening is a wonderful way to engage with nature and spend time alone while nurturing plants.

4) **Mindfulness in Nature:** Practice mindfulness exercises like deep breathing or meditation while sitting in a park or by a lake. The natural setting enhances the calming effects of these practices.

5) **Nature Observation:** Spend time observing the natural world around you. Watch the clouds, listen to

the sounds of birds, or simply sit and take in the scenery. This can be incredibly soothing and grounding.

Real-Life Examples of the Benefits of Nature and Solitude

- **Amogh Lila Das:** As a spiritual teacher, Amogh Lila Das often emphasizes the healing power of nature and solitude. His teachings, inspired by the Bhagavad Gita, highlight how spending time in nature can bring clarity and peace.

- **Thich Nhat Hanh:** The Vietnamese Buddhist monk and peace activist advocates for mindfulness and connection with nature. His retreats often include mindful walking in nature, which he believes helps people reconnect with themselves and find inner peace.

- **Jay Shetty:** Former monk Jay Shetty frequently talks about the importance of solitude and nature. He shares how spending time alone and in nature during his monkhood helped him gain profound insights and clarity.

- **Shivani Didi:** Associated with the Brahma Kumari's, Shivani Didi promotes meditation and mindfulness. She often speaks about the benefits of spending time in nature and solitude to enhance spiritual growth and inner peace.

In conclusion, incorporating nature and solitude into your daily life can significantly enhance your mental, emotional, and physical well-being. By taking time to connect with nature and enjoy solitude, you can reduce stress, boost creativity, improve mental health, and gain a deeper understanding of yourself. These practices are simple yet powerful ways to nurture your spiritual growth and find harmony amidst the chaos of everyday life.

Faith in God

What is Faith in God?
Faith in God refers to a deep trust and belief in a higher power, whether it's God, the universe, or any spiritual force that one believes governs life. This faith provides a sense of purpose, comfort, and guidance, especially during challenging times. It's about surrendering to a higher will and finding peace in the belief that everything happens for a reason.

How to Practice Faith in God
1) **Prayer and Worship:** Regular prayer or worship can help you connect with God. It can be done in a formal setting like a church, temple, or mosque, or informally in your own space. Prayer is a way to express gratitude, seek guidance, and find comfort.

2) **Reading Sacred Texts:** Engaging with sacred texts like the Bhagavad Gita, Bible, Quran, or any scripture that resonates with you can deepen your understanding of spiritual principles and strengthen your faith.

3) **Meditation and Contemplation:** Meditation focused on a higher power can foster a deeper spiritual connection. Contemplative practices involve reflecting on spiritual teachings and how they apply to your life.

4) **Community Involvement:** Being part of a faith community can provide support and encouragement. Participating in community services, attending religious gatherings, and sharing experiences with others can reinforce your faith.

5) **Service and Compassion:** Acts of kindness and service to others are expressions of faith in action. Helping those in need, volunteering, and showing compassion are ways to live out your spiritual beliefs.

6) **Gratitude Practices:** Practicing gratitude by acknowledging and appreciating the blessings in your life can strengthen your faith. It shifts focus from what's lacking to what's abundant and positive.

Impact of Faith in God

1) **Emotional Strength:** Faith provides a source of emotional strength and resilience. Believing in a higher power can offer comfort and hope during difficult times, reducing anxiety and stress.

2) **Sense of Purpose:** Faith gives a sense of purpose and direction. It helps individuals understand their place in the world and the meaning behind their experiences, fostering a sense of fulfilment.

3) **Inner Peace:** Trusting in a higher power can bring inner peace. It alleviates the pressure of trying to control everything and encourages acceptance of life's uncertainties.

4) **Moral and Ethical Guidance:** Faith often comes with a set of moral and ethical guidelines. These

principles can guide behaviour, helping individuals make choices aligned with their values and beliefs.

5) **Community and Belonging:** Faith communities provide a sense of belonging and support. Being part of a group that shares similar beliefs can create strong bonds and a supportive network.

How to Integrate Faith in God into Your Daily Life

1) **Daily Prayers:** Set aside time each day for prayer or meditation. This can be a few minutes in the morning or before bed, helping you start or end the day with a sense of peace.

2) **Study Sacred Texts:** Regularly read and reflect on sacred texts. This can be done individually or as part of a study group, deepening your understanding of spiritual teachings.

3) **Join a Faith Community:** Participate in religious services or faith-based groups. This can provide a support system and opportunities for shared worship and community service.

4) **Acts of Service:** Engage in acts of kindness and service. Volunteering and helping others can be powerful expressions of your faith and reinforce your spiritual principles.

5) **Practice Gratitude:** Incorporate gratitude into your daily routine. Thanking God for your blessings, no matter how small, can strengthen your faith and positivity.

6) **Reflect and Contemplate:** Spend time in reflection and contemplation. Think about your experiences,

challenges, and blessings, and how they fit into your spiritual journey.

Real-Life Examples of the Benefits of Faith in God

- **A.C. Bhakti Vedanta Swami Prabhupada:** The founder of the International Society for Krishna Consciousness (ISKCON), emphasized that faith in God means unwavering devotion and trust in Krishna, the Supreme Personality of Godhead. For him, true faith transcends ritualistic practices and is rooted in the sincere and heartfelt chanting of the holy names, selfless service to the Lord, and living a life aligned with the principles of the Bhagavad Gita. Prabhupada believed that faith is demonstrated through consistent spiritual practices, humility, and the desire to serve and please Krishna in every aspect of life.

- **Dalai Lama:** As the spiritual leader of Tibetan Buddhism, the Dalai Lama's faith in compassion and interfaith dialogue has inspired millions. His teachings on kindness and empathy are rooted in his deep faith.

- **Thich Nhat Hanh:** The Vietnamese Buddhist monk's faith in mindfulness and peace has led to global recognition. His practice of engaged Buddhism, which involves applying mindfulness to social action, showcases the impact of faith.

- **Deepak Chopra:** Known for integrating Eastern spirituality with Western science, Chopra's teachings emphasize the power of faith in achieving mind-body wellness and personal transformation.

- **Shivani Didi (Brahma Kumari Shivani):** Her teachings on meditation, positive thinking, and faith in God help individuals transform their lives and find inner peace.

- **Jaya Kishori:** Her discourses on spirituality and devotion have inspired many to deepen their faith and practice moral values.

- **Amogh Lila Das:** He interprets ancient Vedic wisdom, particularly the Bhagavad Gita, in a modern context, focusing on spiritual growth and mindfulness.

- **Jay Shetty:** He blends ancient wisdom with modern-day practicality, helping people navigate life's challenges through mindfulness and personal growth.

- **Vivek Bindra and Kumar Vishwas:** Both inspire countless individuals with their teachings on motivation, spirituality, and personal development.

In conclusion, faith in God offers profound benefits for emotional well-being, moral guidance, and a sense of purpose. By integrating practices like prayer, meditation, community involvement, and acts of service into your daily life, you can strengthen your faith and find deeper meaning and fulfilment. Whether through traditional religious practices or personal spiritual exploration, nurturing your faith can be a powerful force for positive change in your life.

From Rebel to Serenity
"A Journey of Spiritual Transformation"

Chapter - 1
The Charismatic Rebel

Raj was not your typical high school student. Tall and lean, with a confident swagger that turned heads wherever he went, he had a presence that was both intimidating and magnetic. His jet-black hair was always perfectly styled, complementing his dark, mischievous eyes that seemed to sparkle with untamed energy.

Born into a middle-class family in the bustling city of Oakwood, Raj had always been the centre of attention, whether he liked it or not. From a young age, he possessed a charm that made adults smile and peers gravitate towards him. Despite his outward confidence, beneath the surface lay a boy grappling with insecurities and a need for validation.

In school, Raj was known as the charismatic rebel who could effortlessly charm his way out of trouble. His locker was a shrine to adventure, adorned with stickers of his favorite rock bands and posters of sports heroes. Raj's circle of friends was diverse, ranging from fellow troublemakers who admired his audacity to quieter students who were drawn to his outgoing personality.

One sunny afternoon, Raj sauntered into school late, casually tossing his bag onto his desk as Mr. Singh's lecture droned on about algebra. His friend Sameer nudged him, whispering, "Raj, you missed a regular assessment quiz!"

Raj grinned mischievously. "Who needs algebra when you've got charisma?" he quipped, earning chuckles from the boys around him and amused glances from the girls.

Ignoring Mr. Singh's disapproving stare, Raj spent the rest of the class cracking jokes and passing notes, completely unfazed by the lesson at hand.

Girls were drawn to Raj like moths to a flame. His easy smile and confident demeanour made him irresistible, and he relished the attention they showered upon him. Raj enjoyed flirting and teasing, but he kept his romantic entanglements casual, wary of getting too emotionally involved.

During lunch break, Raj and his friends commandeered a corner table in the cafeteria, where they held court over the latest gossip and sports news. Raj's booming laughter could be heard across the room as he regaled his audience with exaggerated tales of weekend escapades.

"Raj, you're such a legend," Simran, one of the girls in their group, teased, batting her eyelashes playfully. "How do you manage to get away with everything?"

Raj flashed her a cocky grin. "It's all about finesse, Simran," he replied, twirling a French fry between his fingers.

His friends laughed and nodded in agreement, impressed by Raj's ability to turn even the mundane into a spectacle.

Despite his popularity, Raj's academic record was less than stellar. He often found himself bored in class, preferring to crack jokes and entertain his friends rather than focus on algebra or history. Teachers labelled him as a bright student with untapped potential, frustrated by his lack of interest in traditional subjects.

It was a typical Monday morning at Oakwood High School, with students shuffling into Mr. Sharma's history class and settling into their seats. Raj swaggered in a few minutes late, his usual grin in place as he greeted his friends with a casual nod.

Mr. Sharma, a middle-aged teacher known for his patience and dedication, glanced up from his desk with a sigh as Raj took his seat at the back of the room.

"Raj," Mr. Sharma began, his voice tinged with concern, "you missed the last assignment deadline again."

Raj shrugged nonchalantly, leaning back in his chair. "Sorry, sir," he replied with a half-hearted grin. "Got caught up with stuff over the weekend."

Mr. Sharma's disappointment was evident. "Raj, you're capable of so much more," he said earnestly, gesturing towards the stack of papers on his desk. "Your essays show flashes of brilliance, but your inconsistency is holding you back."

Raj glanced away, a flicker of annoyance crossing his face. "Yeah, I know," he muttered, tapping his pencil against the desk. "Just not really into history, you know?"

Mr. Sharma leaned forward; his voice gentle yet firm. "History isn't just about dates and events, Raj. It's about understanding how the past shapes our present and future. Your perspective matters, but you have to apply yourself."

Raj nodded, though his attention seemed to wander. Mr. Sharma sighed inwardly, recognizing the challenge of reaching a student who seemed more interested in socializing than studying.

"Think about it, Raj," Mr. Sharma added quietly before turning back to the whiteboard to begin the day's lesson.

Raj slouched in his seat, the weight of Mr. Sharma's disappointment settling on his shoulders. He knew he had the potential to excel academically, but finding the motivation was a constant struggle amidst the distractions and allure of teenage rebellion.

At home, Raj's relationship with his family was complex. His parents, hardworking and strict, often struggled to understand their son's rebellious streak. They wanted the best for him, pushing him to excel academically and behave responsibly. Raj, in turn, chafed against their expectations, craving freedom and independence.

As Raj navigated the challenges of adolescence, he grappled with questions of identity, purpose, and the desire to carve out his own path in a world that often felt suffocatingly conventional.

Chapter - 2
The Price of Rebellion

The tension between the Red and Blue Houses had been simmering for weeks, ever since the annual inter-house competition had ended in a narrow victory for the Red House. Accusations of cheating and unfair play circulated among the Blue House students, creating a palpable divide. The school grounds were abuzz with rumours, and unease hung in the air.

Raj, always at the centre of attention, had been in high spirits. Despite his rowdy behaviour and disregard for rules, he had a knack for leading his friends and was often seen as the unofficial leader of the Red House. His charisma and fearless attitude attracted many admirers, especially among the girls, but it also made him a target for those who resented his boldness.

The tension between the Red and Blue Houses had reached a boiling point. Rumours of sabotage and cheating had spread like wildfire, and the school's atmosphere was charged with suspicion and anger. Raj, as usual, was right in the thick of things.

It was lunchtime when the incident occurred. Raj and his friends were gathered near the basketball court, their voices carrying across the school grounds as they plotted their next adventure. Raj had come up with a particularly audacious plan: they would shatter one of the large glass windows of the Blue House's common room. It was a reckless idea, born out of a desire to assert their dominance and create chaos.

"Are you sure about this, Raj?" one of his friends asked, a hint of doubt in his voice.

Raj grinned, his eyes gleaming with mischief. "Of course, man! It'll be legendary. They'll be talking about this for weeks."

His friends exchanged uneasy glances but ultimately went along with the plan. Raj's confidence was contagious, and they didn't want to seem cowardly in front of him.

As the group approached the Blue House, Raj took charge, assigning roles to each of his friends. "You two keep watch. The rest of you, follow me."

With the plan set, they moved into position. Raj picked up a large rock and, with a quick glance to ensure the coast was clear, hurled it at the window. The glass shattered with a deafening crash, sending shards flying everywhere. The boys scattered, their hearts pounding with a mix of adrenaline and fear.

As they regrouped at their usual hangout spot, Raj's friends congratulated him, their initial doubts forgotten. "That was epic, Raj! You really pulled it off."

Raj smirked, basking in the praise. "I told you it would be. Now let's see how the Blue House reacts."

Panic ensued as students rushed to see what had happened. Teachers quickly arrived at the scene, trying to control the chaos. The principal, Mr. Kumar, soon appeared, his stern faces a clear indication that this was a serious matter.

"Everyone, back to your classrooms immediately!" Mr. Kumar's voice boomed over the din. "We will investigate this incident thoroughly."

The students reluctantly dispersed, whispering and speculating about what had transpired. Raj and his friends, however, lingered a bit longer, their faces pale and nervous. They knew that this could lead to severe consequences.

Later that day, an announcement was made over the school intercom. "All students of the Red House, please report to the assembly hall immediately."

Raj's heart sank as he made his way to the hall. He had a sinking feeling that this was about the broken window. As he entered, he saw the entire Red House gathered, along with Mr. Kumar and Mr. Sharma, one of the senior teachers known for his fair judgment.

"Students," Mr. Kumar began, "we have reason to believe that the incident involving the Blue House common room window was not an accident. We will be conducting an investigation to find out who is responsible."

Mr. Sharma stepped forward, his calm demeanour a stark contrast to the tension in the room. "We understand that tensions have been high recently, but this kind of behaviour is unacceptable. We will be speaking with each of you to get to the bottom of this."

One by one, the students were called for questioning. Raj's turn finally came, and he walked into the small office where Mr. Sharma sat waiting.

"Raj, please have a seat," Mr. Sharma said kindly. Raj sat down, his mind racing with thoughts of what to say.

"Raj, can you tell me where you were when the window was broken?" Mr. Sharma asked, looking directly at him.

Raj hesitated, knowing that lying would only make things worse. "I was near the basketball court with my friends."

Mr. Sharma nodded, taking notes. "Did you see anyone near the Blue House common room?"

Raj shook his head. "No, sir. I didn't see anyone."

After a few more questions, Raj was dismissed. He left the office feeling a mix of fear and relief. He knew that the truth would eventually come out.

The next day, the school was abuzz with the news that Raj had been found guilty. Mr. Sharma had conducted a thorough investigation, and it turned out that Raj and his friends had been seen near the Blue House common room shortly before the window was broken. Witnesses had come forward, and the evidence was damning.

Mr. Kumar called Raj to his office. "Raj, we have all the evidence we need. You and your friends were involved in the incident. This behaviour cannot be tolerated."

Raj's heart pounded in his chest. He knew that expulsion was a real possibility. "Sir, I'm sorry. It was an accident. We didn't mean for it to happen."

Mr. Kumar sighed, his expression stern. "Accident or not, Raj, this kind of behaviour has consequences. We have no choice but to recommend your expulsion to the school board."

Raj felt his world crumbling around him. The thought of being expelled, of disappointing his family, was too much to bear. Just as he was about to leave the office, Mr. Sharma spoke up.

"Mr. Kumar, if I may," he said, his voice calm and measured. "I believe that expulsion may not be the best solution here."

Mr. Kumar looked surprised. "What do you suggest, Mr. Sharma?"

"I've spoken with Raj, and while his actions were wrong, I see potential in him. He's a bright young man who's lost his way. I believe that with the right guidance, he can turn things around," Mr. Sharma explained.

Mr. Kumar considered this for a moment. "Are you willing to take responsibility for him, Mr. Sharma?"

"Yes, I am," Mr. Sharma replied firmly. "I will mentor Raj and ensure that he understands the gravity of his actions and the importance of making better choices."

Raj looked at Mr. Sharma, stunned by his support. "Thank you, sir," he said, his voice filled with genuine gratitude.

Mr. Kumar nodded. "Very well. Raj, you will be on probation under Mr. Sharma's mentorship. Any further incidents, and you will be expelled immediately. Do you understand?"

"Yes, sir. I understand," Raj replied, relief washing over him.

As Raj left the office, he couldn't help but feel a sense of hope. For the first time, he realized that someone believed in him, despite his mistakes.

Chapter - 3
Guiding Light

Raj had never felt so confused and restless in his life. Mr. Rao had saved him from expulsion, and now he was assigned as Raj's mentor. But days went by, and Mr. Rao made no attempt to reach out. The lack of communication gnawed at Raj. He had expected lectures, perhaps even punishment, but the silence was unnerving.

One evening, as Raj was sitting in his room, trying to focus on his homework, the question that had been haunting him finally burst forth. Why had Mr. Rao saved him? Why was he assigned as his mentor and then left him in the dark?

Unable to bear the uncertainty any longer, Raj decided to take matters into his own hands. The next day after school, he waited outside Mr. Rao's office, his heart pounding with a mix of fear and curiosity. When Mr. Rao finally appeared, Raj took a deep breath and stepped forward.

"Sir, can I talk to you for a minute?" Raj asked, his voice trembling slightly.

Mr. Rao looked at him, a hint of a smile playing on his lips. "Of course, Raj. Come in."

As they settled into the chairs in Mr. Rao's office, Raj blurted out, "Why did you save me? I was guilty. You knew it."

Mr. Rao leaned back in his chair, studying Raj carefully before speaking. "Raj, I don't judge people by their actions alone. I try to look deeper, to see the person behind the mistakes. And in you, I saw potential."

Raj was taken aback. No one had ever spoken to him like this before. "But I've always been a troublemaker. Why would you see potential in me?"

Mr. Rao leaned forward; his eyes earnest. "Because I believe everyone has the capacity for change. It's not about where you are now, but where you can go. I saw a spark in you, Raj. You just need guidance to channel it in the right direction."

This conversation marked the beginning of a series of meetings between Raj and Mr. Rao. At first, Raj was hesitant and guarded, but gradually, he began to open up. Mr. Rao's calm demeanour and genuine interest in his well-being made Raj feel seen and understood for the first time.

In their sessions, Mr. Rao shared his own experiences, revealing that he too had faced significant challenges. "Life hasn't always been easy for me either, Raj. But spirituality helped me stay grounded. It taught me to see beyond immediate problems and understand the bigger picture."

Raj listened intently, intrigued by this new perspective. "What do you mean by spirituality, sir? Is it about religion?"

Mr. Rao shook his head. "Not necessarily. Spirituality is about understanding yourself and your place in the world. It's about finding inner peace and strength, no matter what life throws at you."

Over time, Mr. Rao introduced Raj to various spiritual practices. They talked about meditation, mindfulness, and the teachings of various spiritual leaders. One day, Mr. Rao handed Raj a book.

"This is the Bhagavad Gita," Mr. Rao said. "It's a spiritual classic that has guided many through difficult times. I think you'll find it enlightening."

Raj took the book, feeling a mix of curiosity and scepticism. As he began to read, he found the language challenging, but the ideas fascinating. The conversations with Mr. Rao helped him make sense of the text. One particular shloka caught his attention: "You have the right to perform your duties, but you are not entitled to the fruits of your actions."

"What does this mean, sir?" Raj asked during one of their meetings.

"It means that you should focus on doing your best without worrying about the outcome," Mr. Rao explained. "Detach yourself from the results, and you'll find peace and clarity in your actions."

This idea resonated deeply with Raj. He realized that much of his frustration stemmed from his obsession with outcomes and the opinions of others. Inspired by this new perspective, he began to incorporate spiritual practices into his daily routine.

Raj started with simple mindfulness exercises, paying attention to his breath and staying present in the moment. He practiced meditation, guided by Mr. Rao's teachings. Slowly, he felt a shift within himself. The anger and restlessness that had once defined him began to dissipate, replaced by a sense of calm and focus.

Raj's transformation was slow and steady. However, there were days when his old habits crept back, bringing with them bouts of anger and restlessness. One such day, after a particularly heated argument with a classmate, Raj found himself in front of Mr. Rao's office, seeking solace and answers.

As Raj knocked on the door, Mr. Rao's calm voice invited him in. "Come in, Raj. Sit down."

Raj slumped into a chair; his frustration evident. "Sir, I don't understand. I've been trying so hard to change, but sometimes I just can't control my anger. It's like I know what I should do, but I still end up doing the opposite. Does the Bhagavad Gita talk about this kind of thing?"

Mr. Rao nodded, his eyes kind. "Yes, Raj, it does. The Bhagavad Gita addresses the inner conflicts we all face. It's natural to struggle with anger and restlessness. Even the greatest warriors and sages have battled these emotions."

Raj looked up, a flicker of hope in his eyes. "Really? What does it say about anger?"

Mr. Rao opened a worn copy of the Bhagavad Gita and turned to a specific page. "There's a shloka that speaks directly to this. It's Chapter 2, Verse 62-63:

'ध्यायतो विषयान्पुंस: सङ्गस्तेषूपजायते |
सङ्गात्सञ्जायते काम: कामात्क्रोधोऽभिजायते ||

क्रोधाद्भवति सम्मोह: सम्मोहात्स्मृतिविभ्रम: |
स्मृतिभ्रंशाद् बुद्धिनाशो बुद्धिनाशात्प्रणश्यति ||

'While contemplating the objects of the senses, a person develops attachment for them, and from such attachment lust develops, and from lust anger arises.

From anger, complete delusion arises, and from delusion bewilderment of memory. When memory is bewildered, intelligence is lost, and when intelligence is lost, one falls down again into the material pool.'

Raj listened intently, the meaning of the shloka slowly sinking in. "So, it all starts with attachment?"

Mr. Rao nodded. "Yes. When we become attached to certain outcomes or desires, we set ourselves up for disappointment and frustration. That frustration often manifests as anger. The key is to practice detachment – to perform your duties without getting attached to the results."

"But how do I do that?" Raj asked, genuinely curious.

Mr. Rao smiled. "It's a lifelong practice, Raj. It involves mindfulness and self-awareness. The first step is recognizing the emotions as they arise. When you feel anger bubbling up, take a step back and observe it. Don't judge it, just acknowledge it. Ask yourself why you're feeling this way. What attachment or desire is causing this anger?"

Raj took a deep breath, trying to absorb the advice. "I guess I get angry when things don't go my way or when someone challenges me."

"Exactly," Mr. Rao said. "It's the attachment to control and the fear of losing it. By practicing detachment, you learn to accept things as they are, without trying to force them to be a certain way."

Raj nodded slowly. "That makes sense. But it's so hard to control. Sometimes I feel like I'm fighting myself."

Mr. Rao leaned forward; his expression serious. "That's because you are. The Bhagavad Gita also talks about the dual nature of the mind. Arjuna, the warrior prince, faced a similar dilemma on the battlefield. He knew what was right but felt overwhelmed by his emotions. Krishna, his charioteer, and guide, told him that this internal battle is a part of life. The mind can be our best friend or our worst enemy. The goal of spiritual practice is to train the mind to be our ally."

Raj looked thoughtful. "How do I train my mind?"

"Through regular practice of mindfulness, meditation, and reflection," Mr. Rao replied. "Start with small steps. When you feel anger or restlessness, take a few deep breaths. Remind yourself of your goal to remain calm and cantered. Over time, you'll find it easier to manage these emotions."

Raj felt a sense of relief. For the first time, he felt like he had a concrete strategy to deal with his inner turmoil. "Thank you, sir. This really helps."

Mr. Rao smiled warmly. "I'm glad, Raj. Remember, it's a journey. Be patient with yourself. And whenever you feel overwhelmed, don't hesitate to come and talk to me."

Raj left Mr. Rao's office feeling lighter. He had a long way to go, but with Mr. Rao's guidance and the wisdom of the Bhagavad Gita, he felt more equipped to face his struggles. As he walked through the school corridors, he resolved to practice what he had learned, one step at a time. The path to inner peace was challenging, but Raj was determined to walk it, with Mr. Rao and the teachings of spirituality as his guiding lights.

He also started reading other spiritual texts recommended by Mr. Rao, like "The Art of Happiness" by the Dalai Lama and "The Power of Now" by Eckhart Tolle. These books reinforced the principles he was learning and provided practical advice on living a more balanced and meaningful life.

As Raj's spiritual journey progressed, so did his transformation. His grades improved, and he became more disciplined and focused. Teachers who had once written him off as a troublemaker began to notice the change and praised his efforts.

One day, after a particularly insightful session, Raj turned to Mr. Rao and said, "You've changed my life, sir. I never thought I could feel this way. Calm, focused, and... happy."

Mr. Rao smiled warmly. "You did the hard work, Raj. I just showed you the path. Remember, spirituality is a lifelong journey. Keep learning, keep growing."

Raj nodded, feeling a deep sense of gratitude. He realized that his journey was just beginning, but with Mr. Rao's guidance and the principles of spirituality, he felt ready to face whatever challenges lay ahead.

This newfound perspective not only transformed Raj's life but also inspired those around him. His friends noticed the change and began to ask him about his experiences. Raj eagerly shared what he had learned, encouraging them to explore spirituality for themselves.

Through his journey, Raj discovered that true strength and confidence come from within. He learned to value relationships, approach challenges with a calm mind, and most importantly, understand and accept himself. Raj's story became a testament to the power of spirituality in transforming lives and finding inner peace amidst the chaos of the world.

Bhagavad Geeta
"A Timeless Wisdom"

Like most kids of your generation, I also thought of the Bhagavad Gita as just a religious book. That was until I started reading it.

The Gita being labelled merely as a religious text limit its reach, which is truly unfortunate. Long before Twitter threads talked about our biggest enemy being within, the Gita had already covered it. Much before movies talked about the fleeting nature of wealth, the Gita had discussed it (Moh Maaya). Before health bloggers emphasized yoga, the Gita had done it and went further to include Gyan yoga, bhakti yoga, and karma yoga. When modern advice tells you to face your fears and avoid self-pity, the Gita has those lessons too.

Every day, we are fighting our own battles, much like the battle of Kurukshetra between the Kauravas and Pandavas. The Gita challenges us to set our ego aside and see things differently. Imagine your life without past memories haunting you or without the need for social validation. Would a friend's happy Instagram post still make you feel insecure about your own life? Instead of looking for answers from your favourite online personalities, maybe read the Bhagavad Gita instead.

Beyond all this, the Gita has taught me that our role in life changes every day. Sometimes, we are the charioteer, Krishna, pulling the reins. Other times, we are Arjun, needing that extra push to realize our worth. And some days, we might feel like one of the Kauravas, blinded by our ego. It's a struggle, a battle not outside on the battlefield but within us. You've probably heard it many times: it's not about winning or losing; it's about discovering yourself in the process. Guess who said it much before reality shows? The Bhagavad Gita.

Instead of the usual morning WhatsApp forward for inspiration, just pick up the Bhagavad Gita.

Today's youth face multiple emotional challenges due to various factors such as diminishing value systems, crumbling family structures, and lack of quality education. Uncontrolled access to technology has further exacerbated these issues. Adolescents often struggle to differentiate right from wrong and can easily fall into the trap of the virtual world created by the Internet and other forms of technology. They lack patience and develop behavioural issues like a decreasing sense of responsibility, attention deficit, excessive anger, tech dependence, drug abuse, open defiance, and an 'I don't care' attitude. Some parents, trying to placate their children by providing them with everything, inadvertently worsen the problem. The pressure on kids to excel in everything they do can be too much, hindering natural growth and leading to various behavioural issues. The deviant behaviour of teenagers is increasingly becoming a cause for concern in society.

The concerns of increasingly restless and perpetually dissatisfied young minds can be addressed, and the strength of their character built if the teachings of ancient Indian scriptures like the Bhagavad Gita are inculcated in them. The Gita contains rich and unfathomable words of wisdom, which can be appreciated by today's youth if its practical aspects are presented in a relatable and digestible manner. Knowledge from the Gita, thus, has to be made available to kids in an interesting and engaging way, helping them prepare to cope with challenges they face or are likely to face in the future.

The Gita is a guidebook to life. It teaches us not to run away from life's struggles and to work hard without worrying about the results. The doctrine of karma (the law of cause and effect) – as one sows, so shall he reap – can motivate everyone to do good. The Gita teaches the equanimity of mind. Teaching children to accept failure with grace is as important as teaching them to handle success with humility. This understanding can help them reduce anxiety levels and avoid emotional outbursts, enhancing their ability to cope with different situations.

According to the Bhagavad Gita, the mind is a powerful instrument through which one can rise to great heights or fall to immeasurable depths. The mind is the best friend of those who have conquered it, but it proves to be the worst enemy of one who fails to control it. If the message of self-restraint and self-discipline is instilled early on, one can face all challenges of life boldly.

The Gita emphasizes the importance of anger management. Lust, greed, jealousy, and fear are considered the worst enemies of man. By keeping such vices in check, one can obtain serenity of mind and thus flourish in life. The concentration of mind taught in the Gita is quite helpful for students in channelizing their energies toward achieving their goals. The Bhagavad Gita preaches the unity of the Divine and the oneness of mankind. If such a concept is understood at a young age, one becomes more humane, with feelings of love, empathy, trust, and kindness arising naturally. When a child understands that there is only one Supreme Power, they start respecting every religion.

The Gita also declares that excess of everything is bad. Too much eating, fasting, waking, or sleeping is not good, and one should not indulge in too much recreation. Once this principle of moderate behaviour is understood properly, students can establish a proper balance between their studies, sports, and other activities.

The Gita also sheds light on the ideal teacher-pupil relationship. It advises that a student must pay due regard to his teacher but should never hesitate to ask meaningful questions. The teacher must impart full knowledge to his students. It is also stated that an elder should set a good example through his actions for the young ones to follow. However, the teacher must not impose his views on his students. After thinking seriously about the wisdom imparted, students must form their own opinions. In this manner, the teacher can motivate his pupils to realize their full potential.

The Gita is a complex book, with concepts that are not easy for kids to understand. On the first reading, they may not make much sense, as the text and its meanings are quite subtle. Therefore, it is the duty of parents, teachers, and other elders to identify lessons relevant to kids and then explain them in language appropriate to their age.

While imparting knowledge of scriptures, it must be ensured that the formal education of students is not impacted. In short, the Bhagavad Gita is not a treatise to be read by ascetics or senior citizens only. If the basic principles of this timeless guide to meaningful and purposeful living are internalized by the young, it can help them adopt a pragmatic and progressive approach to life.

With the guidance of my spiritual gurus, I have delved deep into the profound wisdom of the Bhagavad Gita. Now, I stand before you, ready to illuminate its teachings in a simpler, more relatable way that resonates with the challenges and realities of our lives today. Together, let's embark on this transformative journey. So, let's begin.

Harish Sir's Gita Insights Navigating Student Life

Mastering Actions: Beyond Results

It was a typical Tuesday afternoon in the school library, the soft hum of students whispering and the occasional rustle of pages creating a comforting background noise. Harish Sir, the beloved teacher known for his profound wisdom and approachable demeanour, was helping a few students with their upcoming exams. Among them was Arjun, a diligent student who, despite his best efforts, seemed unusually anxious.

As Harish Sir moved from one student to the next, offering guidance and encouragement, he noticed Arjun staring blankly at his notes, his brow furrowed in worry. Sensing something was off, Harish Sir pulled up a chair beside him.

"Hey Arjun," he said gently, "you seem a bit troubled. What's on your mind?"

Arjun looked up, his eyes betraying his concern. "Sir, I'm really struggling to focus. The pressure of the exams is getting to me, and I just can't seem to calm my mind."

From behind, Sujal, another student sitting beside Arjun, suddenly said, "Same with me, sir."

Harish Sir nodded understandingly. "I see. It's completely natural to feel this way, especially with exams looming. But remember, stress and worry won't help you perform better. Let's talk about it."

As the conversation unfolded, other students, intrigued by the discussion, began to gather around. Harish Sir, always eager to share his wisdom, saw an opportunity to impart a valuable life lesson. He began recounting some teachings from the Bhagavad Gita, seamlessly weaving them into the context of their current struggles.

Arjun, still sceptical but hopeful, asked, "Sir, you always give us examples from the Bhagavad Gita. Does this book really have all the solutions to our worries?"

Without hesitation, Harish Sir replied, "Yes, without any doubts." The students leaned in closer, their curiosity piqued. Arjun's eyes lit up, and he said, "Yes, sir, it sounds cool too when you quote shlokas in Sanskrit while guiding us."

Harish Sir smiled warmly. "Yes, it's very cool. There's no cooler book of reference for life than the Gita."

With the students fully engaged, Harish Sir decided to delve deeper into the profound lessons of the Bhagavad Gita, making the ancient wisdom relevant to their modern lives.

Sujal: Sure, but can you make it relatable to us? Sometimes it's hard to grasp ancient texts.

Harish Sir: Of course! Think about Arjuna from the Gita. Like all of us, he was human and faced life's endless pairs of opposites: pleasure and pain, joy and sorrow, profit and loss, victory and defeat, success and failure. We all spend our time chasing the 'good' side and avoiding the 'bad' side, right?

Arjun: Yeah, I always want to avoid failure and loss.

Harish Sir: Here's the thing: both sides are intertwined. You can't have one without the other. It's only because we know pleasure that we recognize pain. It's only because we value success that we fear failure. One defines the other.

Sujal: That makes sense, but it's tough to deal with the bad stuff.

Harish Sir: True. But imagine this: have you ever noticed that when you achieve something without much effort, it doesn't feel as rewarding? Conversely, if you don't deeply care about something, you don't miss it when it's gone. Neither joy nor sorrow, success nor failure lasts forever.

Sujal: So, should we just accept everything as it is?

Harish Sir: Yes, accepting both sides with equanimity is one approach. Another powerful way is to reject both sides. By doing so, you neither get elated by success nor devastated by failure. This brings a sense of calm. And in that calmness, there's no fear of failure, no desperate craving for success, no sorrow over loss, and no anger at rejection.

Arjun: That sounds really hard. How do we even start?

Harish Sir: It is challenging, but you can begin by focusing on the work at hand. Whether it's studying for an exam, helping your parents, or working on a project, immerse yourself fully in the task. Don't think about how unpleasant the work is, don't worry about the results or the rewards. Just do it.

Arjun: But won't that make life boring?

Harish Sir: On the surface, it might seem that way. But those who live this way find it to be a path to perfect and lasting happiness. The work itself becomes the purpose, and you stop seeking rewards outside of it. The work becomes the reward.

Sujal: That's interesting. It reminds me of a poem we read. It talked about treating triumph and disaster the same.

If you can dream - and not make dreams your master;
If you can think - and not make thoughts your aim;
If you can meet with Triumph and Disaster
And treat those two impostors just the same;

If you can talk with crowds and keep your virtue,
Or walk with Kings - nor lose the common touch,
If neither foes nor loving friends can hurt you,
If all men count with you, but none too much;

If you can fill the unforgiving minute
With sixty seconds' worth of distance run,
Yours is the Earth and everything that's in it,
And which is more - you'll be a Man, my son!

Harish Sir: Exactly! Rudyard Kipling's poem "If" captures this philosophy beautifully. If you can meet with Triumph and Disaster and treat those two impostors just the same, you gain a profound understanding of life.

Arjun: So, the Gita's philosophy is about focusing on the journey, not the destination?

Harish Sir: Precisely. If the Gita's teachings were reduced to one verse, it would be Shloka 47 from Chapter 2. It goes:

कर्मण्येवाधिकारस्ते मा फलेषु कदाचन ।
मा कर्मफलहेतुर्भूर्मा ते सङ्गोऽस्त्वकर्मणि ॥

"You only have the right to perform your duty, but you are not entitled to the fruits of your action. Never consider yourself the cause of the results of your activities, and never be attached to inaction."

Arjun: That's powerful. It's like saying just focus on what you can control – your actions – and let go of the rest.

Harish Sir: Exactly. Embrace the journey, perform your duties with dedication, and let go of the attachment to outcomes. This mindset can transform your life, leading to true contentment and inner peace.

Arjun: I see now. It's about finding balance and not letting external factors dictate our happiness.

With this new perspective, the students felt empowered to face their exams and future challenges with confidence and equanimity, armed with the timeless wisdom of the Bhagavad Gita.

The Catalyst for Self-Discipline

It was a typical Tuesday afternoon in the school garden. The sun was shining, and a gentle breeze rustled the leaves. The students had just finished their lunch and were enjoying some free time when they noticed Harish Sir sitting on a bench, reading a book. His calm demeanour always had a way of drawing the students to him. As they gathered around, Rohan couldn't help but blurt out something that had been bothering him.

Rohan: Harish Sir, I'm really stressed out. I have so much homework, and I always end up watching TV instead of doing it. Then, I have to stay up late to finish everything.

Harish Sir put his book down and looked at Rohan with understanding eyes.

Harish Sir: Rohan, you're not alone. A lot of us struggle with managing our time and staying disciplined. Why don't we all sit down and talk about this?

The students quickly found spots on the grass, eager to hear what Harish Sir had to say. Meera and Neha joined the circle, both nodding in agreement with Rohan's problem.

Meera: I feel the same way. I start doing my homework, but then I get distracted by my phone. Before I know it, hours have passed, and I haven't done much.

Neha: I know! I promised myself I'd practice my music every day, but I keep putting it off.

Harish Sir smiled, seeing a perfect opportunity to teach a valuable lesson.

Harish Sir: Alright, gang, let's chat about something super important today. Self-discipline. Who knows what that is?

Rohan: Is it like when we have to do our homework on time?

Harish Sir: Exactly, Rohan! Self-discipline is like a muscle. The more you exercise it, the stronger it gets. It's what keeps us in great emotional shape.

Neha: But, Harish Sir, why is self-discipline so important?

Harish Sir: Good question, Neha. Self-discipline is at the root of a happy, healthy, stress-free life. It's not just about big things like exercising or meditating. It's the small stuff, like limiting TV time on school nights, brushing your teeth before bed, or not finishing an entire pack of chips in one go.

Aashna: But no one can force us to do these things, right?

Harish Sir: Right, Aashna. Self-discipline isn't something anyone can impose on you. It's something you impose on yourself because you can see the benefits clearly. For example, if you watch only half an hour of TV, you have time left to play and do your homework, which makes you happy. Brushing your teeth saves you scary trips to the dentist. Not finishing that pack of chips means you can eat something healthier later.

Meera: So, it's like creating good habits?

Harish Sir: Yes, Meera. Kids who pack their school bags the night before grow into teens who practice their music daily, who grow into college students who don't drink and drive, and eventually into adults who exercise regularly and balance work with family time. Do you see the pattern?

Rohan: It's like a habit that gets stronger over time.

Harish Sir: Exactly, Rohan! Self-discipline is a habit, not something you're born with, which means anyone can cultivate it. The more you practice it, the easier it gets.

Aashna: But it's so hard to stick to it!

Harish Sir: True, Aashna. Even Arjuna in the Bhagavad Gita acknowledges how difficult it is. In Chapter 6, Verse 6, Arjuna says:

योऽयं योगस्त्वया प्रोक्तः साम्येन मधुसूदन ।
एतस्याहं न पश्यामि चञ्चलत्वात्स्थितिं स्थिराम् ॥

The system of Yog that you have described, O Madhusudan, appears impractical and unattainable to me, due to the restless mind.

चञ्चलं हि मनः कृष्ण प्रमाथि बलवद्दृढम् ।
तस्याहं निग्रहं मन्ये वायोरिव सुदुष्करम् ॥

The mind is very restless, turbulent, strong and obstinate, O Krishna. It appears to me that it is more difficult to control than the wind.

Aashna: Exactly! So how did Krishna react to this question?

Harish Sir: Krishna's reply was very simple and clear. In the next verse he says:

असंशयं महाबाहो मनो दुर्निग्रहं चलम् ।
अभ्यासेन तु कौन्तेय वैराग्येण च गृह्यते ॥

O mighty-armed son of Kunti, what you say is correct; the mind is indeed very difficult to restrain. But by practice and detachment, it can be controlled.

Neha: But if it's so beneficial, why don't more people practice self-discipline?

Harish Sir: Ah, Neha, that's because the benefits aren't always immediate. If you skip brushing your teeth one night, they won't fall out by morning. Sometimes, the repercussions aren't guaranteed either. But the main reason is that self-discipline is hard. Even Krishna in the Bhagavad Gita acknowledges this.

असंयतात्मना योगी दुष्प्राप इति मे मतिः |
वश्यात्मना तु यतता शक्योऽवाप्तुमुपायतः ||

Yog is difficult to attain for one whose mind is unbridled. However, those who have learnt to control the mind, and who strive earnestly by proper means, can attain perfection in Yog. This is My opinion.

Aashna: So how do we get started?

Harish Sir: Start small. Carve out 15 minutes each day to sit quietly by yourself. Find a quiet, clean place, sit comfortably, and don't slouch. Close your eyes and focus. Krishna suggests focusing on the tip of your nose, but you could focus on anything—just not a TV or Mobile screen!

Meera: What should we think about?

Harish Sir: Keep it simple. Think about things you're grateful for, what you could have done better, or what made you mad or sad. The key is to do this every day at the same time until it becomes a habit. After two weeks, you'll see how proud you feel for sticking to it. Then, start adding other routines—like only eating junk food on weekends, tidying up your desk twice a week, or reading new books regularly.

Rohan: It sounds like it could make us feel really good about ourselves.

Harish Sir: Exactly! Your self-esteem will soar, you'll tackle tough challenges fearlessly, and you'll be a more confident, happier person.

Neha: That's awesome, Harish Sir! What's not to like about that?

Harish Sir: Nothing at all, Neha. So, who's ready to start their self-discipline journey?

The students nodded enthusiastically, inspired to build their self-discipline muscle and see where it could take them.

Embracing Responsibility

It was the end of the school day, and the students were slowly gathering their things to head home. Harish Sir, always a comforting presence, was sitting under the big banyan tree where the students often congregated for casual chats. Today, however, there was a sense of unrest among them. They seemed troubled and confused.

Aisha: Harish Sir, we were talking about how hard it is to handle responsibility. It feels like such a heavy burden.

Harish Sir looked around at the earnest faces and smiled gently.

Harish Sir: Responsibility is indeed a big word, Aisha. But it's important to understand what it truly means. It's not quite the same as duty. Duty is something you are obliged to do, something you could be punished for not doing. But responsibility is an option. No rule says you have to take it, and no one can punish you for not taking it. Yet, according to the Gita and any good person's code of living, your responsibility, however unpleasant it may be, is just as sacred as your duty.

Rohan: So, doing our homework and being respectful to teachers are our duties, right?

Harish Sir: Exactly, Rohan. As students, those are your duties. But let's say you're great at maths and you've promised to help a friend who struggles with it after school. Keeping that promise is your responsibility.

Neha: What about standing up to a bully, even if the bully is your friend? Is that a responsibility too?

Harish Sir: Yes, Neha. As members of the school community, it's our responsibility to intervene when we see someone being bullied. And as a school prefect, being a role model by being punctual, disciplined, and respectful is your responsibility, even when no one is watching.

Meera: But responsibilities are hard. We often try to avoid them, especially when they're unpleasant.

Harish Sir: True, Meera. Duties are often done out of fear of reprimand, but responsibilities, without such fear attached, are easy to shirk off. For instance, standing up to a close friend because you don't approve of their behaviour can be very unpleasant, so we often reject that responsibility.

Aisha: And then we feel guilty for not doing what we knew was right.

Harish Sir: Exactly. We make excuses like, 'It's not my problem,' or 'I don't want to hurt my friend,' but these are just that—excuses. The real trouble is that letting yourself off the hook becomes a habit, and 'It's not my problem' could become your life motto. And that would be a shame.

Rohan: We wouldn't want to grow up into people who ignore someone in need or overlook unethical behaviour just because it's not our problem.

Harish Sir: Right, Rohan. Imagine being the person who sees someone injured on the road but drives away because they think, 'It's not my problem.' Or a businessperson who overlooks child labour because they think, 'It's not my problem.' Or a homemaker who ignores their cook's domestic issues because 'what happens in her house is not my problem.'

Neha: It's like in the Mahabharata, right? Arjuna had a huge responsibility to fight for what was right, even though it meant going against his family.

Harish Sir: Yes, Neha. Arjuna's situation was far tougher than most we will face. His responsibility as a leader and a righteous person was to stand up to unrighteousness and protect the people, even if it meant fighting his own family. In the Gita, Krishna reminds Arjuna that responsibilities are sacred.

अथ चेत्त्वमिमं धर्म्यं संग्रामं न करिष्यसि |
तत: स्वधर्मं कीर्तिं च हित्वा पापमवाप्स्यसि ||

If, however, you refuse to fight this righteous war, abandoning your social duty and reputation, you will certainly incur sin.

सुखदु:खे समे कृत्वा लाभालाभौ जयाजयौ |
ततो युद्धाय युज्यस्व नैवं पापमवाप्स्यसि ||

Fight for the sake of duty, treating alike happiness and distress, loss and gain, victory and defeat. Fulfilling your responsibility in this way, you will never incur sin.

Aisha: So, even if we don't like our responsibilities, we should still embrace them because it's the right thing to do.

Harish Sir: Absolutely, Aisha. Responsibilities shape us into better individuals. By shouldering them, we grow stronger and more resilient. Remember, it's not about the fear of punishment but about understanding the sacredness of our responsibilities and the positive impact they have on our lives and others.

The students nodded thoughtfully, feeling a new found sense of clarity and determination. Harish Sir's words resonated deeply, reminding them of the importance of embracing their responsibilities with courage and integrity.

Faith - Beyond Doubt

It was a rainy afternoon, and the students were gathered in the cosy library of their school. The soft sound of raindrops tapping against the windows created a calming atmosphere. The students had been working on their assignments but were now taking a break, lounging on the bean bags and chatting about their dreams and the obstacles they faced.

Aisha: (sighing) Sometimes, it feels so hard to believe in our dreams, especially when things don't go our way.

Rohan: Yeah, like when we put in so much effort and still don't see any results. It's really discouraging.

Harish Sir, who had been sitting quietly in a corner, reading a book, overheard the conversation. He closed his book, smiled, and decided to join the students. He could see they needed some guidance and encouragement.

Harish Sir: Hey everyone, mind if I join in?

Meera: Of course not, Harish Sir! We were just talking about how tough it is to keep faith in our dreams.

Harish Sir settled down comfortably among the students on the soft bean bags.

Harish Sir: I understand, Aisha. It's not uncommon to feel that way. But let me tell you a little secret about achieving anything worthwhile in life. It all starts with faith. Think about it—anyone who has achieved anything significant did so because they had faith. They believed in an idea, in themselves, or in a higher power.

Neha: But how do we keep that faith, Harish Sir? Especially when everything seems to be going wrong?

Harish Sir looked around at the students, all of them eager for answers. He knew this was the perfect moment to share some wisdom with them.

Harish Sir: Let me share a few stories with you. These are about people who faced incredible challenges but never lost faith. Take Madame Curie, for instance. She believed that a mineral called pitchblende, which was mostly uranium, contained something else as well. Despite facing numerous challenges, she spent 15 years tirelessly working to separate that 'something else'— which she named Radium. Her faith and perseverance proved her right.

Rohan: Wow, 15 years! That's a long time to keep believing in something.

Harish Sir: It is, Rohan. But her faith was unwavering. And she backed it up with hard work and self-discipline. Consider Sister Teresa, who later became known as Mother Teresa. She felt a calling from God to leave her convent and help the poor. Despite doubts and hardships, including begging for food, she persisted. Her faith and dedication led her to establish the Missionaries of Charity, serving the poorest of the poor, and eventually earning her the Nobel Peace Prize.

Meera: That's so inspiring! But what about someone more recent?

Harish Sir: Well, there's J.K. Rowling. She believed so strongly in her story about a boy wizard that she didn't give up, even after 17 publishers rejected her manuscript. The 18th publisher took a chance, and today, Harry Potter is one of the most beloved characters worldwide.

Aisha: But how do we keep faith when things are so tough?

Harish Sir: Great question, Aisha. It's essential to remember that faith is not just about believing but also about putting in the work. Krishna in the Bhagavad Gita says:

कर्मण्येवाधिकारस्ते मा फलेषु कदाचन |
मा कर्मफलहेतुर्भूर्मा ते सङ्गोऽस्त्वकर्मणि ||

You have a right to perform your prescribed duties, but you are not entitled to the fruits of your actions. Never consider yourself to be the cause of the results of your activities, nor be attached to inaction.

We must perform our duties with dedication and without expectation of reward. This requires self-discipline, sacrifice, and a lot of hard work.

Neha: That sounds tough, but I guess it makes sense.

Harish Sir: It is tough, Neha. But it's also rewarding. Self-discipline means sometimes giving up what's easy, like watching TV, to do what's necessary, like writing or studying. It means making sacrifices, like skipping a movie with friends to finish your work. But through these efforts, you gain wisdom and clarity.

Rohan: How does this discipline connect with faith?

Harish Sir: Discipline and faith are intertwined, Rohan. Faith gives you the strength to start, and discipline keeps you going. When you believe in something deeply, whether it's a goal or a higher purpose, you find the motivation to work towards it consistently. And as you build discipline, your faith strengthens because you see the progress you're making.

If we had to put it down as a mathematical equation, it would look something like this:

Faith + Self-discipline* = Wisdom Happiness

Where, Self-discipline = Sacrifice + Hard Work

&

Happiness = No Doubts + No Fear

Meera: Can you share an example from your own life, Harish Sir?

Harish Sir: Of course, Meera. When I was your age, I struggled with managing my time. I loved reading comics and would often lose track of time, neglecting my studies. It was only when I decided to set specific times for reading and studying that I started to see a change. It wasn't easy, but with persistence, it became a habit. And that discipline helped me in many areas of my life.

Aisha: This makes a lot of sense, Harish Sir. Thank you for explaining it so well.

Harish Sir: You're welcome, Aisha. Remember, every small step counts. Keep the faith, stay disciplined, and you'll see great things happen. Keep Faith on Krishna or whatever you call in has the highest power - He is a silent guardian, a watchful protector, a dark knight. And also, Krishna himself promises in the Gita,

मन्मना भव मद्भक्तो मद्याजी मां नमस्कुरु |
मामेवैष्यसि सत्यं ते प्रतिजाने प्रियोऽसि मे ||

Always think of Me, become My devotee, worship Me, offer your homage unto Me and keep faith on me. Thus, you will come to Me without fail. I promise you this because you are My very dear friend.

This shloka emphasizes the importance of faith and righteousness, no matter how difficult the path.

Rohan: So, with faith and hard work, we can achieve our dreams?

Harish Sir: Absolutely, Rohan. With faith, self-discipline, and hard work, you'll gain wisdom and overcome doubts and fears. This combination is a recipe for happiness and success. Keep the faith, work hard, and remember that every challenge is an opportunity to grow.

Aisha: This makes a lot of sense, Harish Sir. Thank you for explaining it so well.

The students nodded thoughtfully, feeling inspired and more confident in their abilities. Harish Sir's words resonated deeply, reminding them that faith, backed by effort and discipline, could help them achieve their dreams.

Ride of Life

The final bell of the day had just rung, and the students of Class 10 gathered their things, eager to head to the sports field where their school team was playing a crucial match against a rival school. As they hurried towards the field, their faces were filled with excitement and anticipation. Harish Sir, their favourite mentor, was accompanying them, known for his inspiring talks that often left the students motivated.

As they reached the sports field, cheers erupted from the stands where their school's supporters were already in full voice. The match had been intense, and until now, their school team had been leading. Aisha, Rohan, and Neha, among the loudest in their cheers, were passionately rooting for their team.

Aisha: (cheering loudly) Come on, team! You've got this!

Rohan: (pumping his fist) That's it! Keep pushing!

Neha: (clapping enthusiastically) We're going to win this!

Harish Sir, standing beside them, smiled as he watched their enthusiasm. However, as the game progressed, their school team began to face tough opposition. The opponents started gaining momentum, and soon, the score started tilting against their school team. The cheers from their supporters began to fade as disappointment crept in.

Aisha: (frowning) Oh no, they were doing so well!

Rohan: (looking concerned) We can't lose this match now!

Neha: (biting her lip) Come on, team, you can still turn this around!

Harish Sir, sensing their disappointment, gathered the students close.

Harish Sir: It's not over yet, guys. Remember what we discussed earlier about the ups and downs in life? This match is a lot like that roller coaster. Our team might be facing a tough phase now, but how they handle this situation matters just as much as their earlier success.

The students nodded, listening intently to Harish Sir's words of wisdom.

Aisha: Harish Sir, I think, just like this match how unpredictable life is. It also feels like a roller coaster, and sometimes it's hard to enjoy the ride when things get tough.

Harish Sir's eyes sparkled as he saw the perfect opportunity to share some wisdom.

Harish Sir: That's a great observation, Aisha. Life indeed is like a roller coaster. It has its ups and downs, twists and turns, and just like on a real roller coaster, we often have no control over these changes. But there's something important we need to understand about this analogy.

The students leaned in, eager to hear more.

Harish Sir: On a real roller coaster, you can sit back and enjoy the ride, knowing that you have no control over it. But in the roller coaster of life, each one of us has a job to do. Some of these jobs might seem incredibly important, while others might appear trivial. But no matter what job we have, we can't control the ride itself.

Rohan: So, are you saying our efforts don't matter?

Harish Sir: Not exactly, Rohan. Our mistake often lies in believing that we are in control of the roller coaster's route. We think that by doing our jobs perfectly, we can ensure only ups and avoid the downs. We strive for success, such as coming first in class or winning a tournament, and while these are wonderful goals, sometimes life throws us a curveball despite our best efforts.

The students nodded, beginning to see the wisdom in Harish Sir's words.

Neha: That sounds so frustrating. What's the point of trying then?

Harish Sir: The point, Neha, is that our efforts do matter, just not in the way we might think. Our job isn't to control the roller coaster but to make the ride enjoyable and meaningful for ourselves and our co-passengers. Being a good student, a supportive friend, a caring sibling – these roles might seem small, but they are crucial. They make the ride smoother and less scary for everyone.

Aisha: But what if we get disappointed because we don't get the results we want?

Harish Sir: That's a great question, Aisha. The Bhagavad Gita teaches us to perform our duties without being attached to the results. This means studying hard not to top the class but because it's our duty as students. Helping a friend not because we expect something in return but because it's the right thing to do.

Rohan: So, it's like we should just do our best and leave the rest to the Universe?

Harish Sir: Exactly, Rohan. It's about doing your best in every situation and trusting that the Universe will take care of the rest. This approach reduces stress and helps us stay focused on what truly matters.

Neha: But what about the times when we are tempted to do something wrong, even though we know it's not right?

Harish Sir: That's a very important point, Neha. Even Arjuna asked exactly same question from Krishna why people sometimes do things they know are wrong, as if compelled by some force.

अथ केन प्रयुक्तोऽयं पापं चरति पूरुष: |
अनिच्छन्नपि वार्ष्णेय बलादिव नियोजित: ||

Why is a person impelled to commit sinful acts, even unwillingly, as if by force, O descendent of Vrishni (Krishna)?

Krishna explains that this force is desire and anger, born of passion. These emotions can devour everything and are considered our enemies.

Harish Sir: Here's a shloka from the Gita that explains it beautifully:

काम एष क्रोध एष रजोगुणसमुद्भवः |
महाशनो महापाप्मा विद्ध्येनमिह वैरिणम् ||

it is lust alone, which is born of contact with the mode of passion, and later transformed into anger. Know this as the sinful, all-devouring enemy in the world.

इन्द्रियाणि मनो बुद्धिरस्याधिष्ठानमुच्यते |
एतैर्विमोहयत्येष ज्ञानमावृत्य देहिनम् ||

The senses, mind, and intellect are said to be breeding grounds of desire. Through them, it clouds one's knowledge and deludes the embodied soul.

Aisha: So, we need to control our desires and anger to stay on the right path?

Harish Sir: Yes, Aisha. By being aware of these forces and striving to overcome them, we can stay true to our duties and live a balanced, fulfilling life.

The students sat silently for a moment, absorbing the profound wisdom shared by Harish Sir. They felt inspired and more equipped to handle the roller coaster ride of life.

Harish Sir: Remember, life will always have its ups and downs. You can't control the ride, but you can choose to enjoy it and make it meaningful. Keep faith in your efforts, stay disciplined, and trust that the Universe has a plan for you.

Neha: Thank you, Harish Sir. This conversation has given us a lot to think about.

Harish Sir: You're welcome, Neha. Now, go out there and enjoy the ride. Make the most of every moment and remember to keep faith in yourself and your journey.

Harish Sir sensed that these students were deeply engaged in this conversation. He gently redirected their focus back to the match.

Harish Sir: This is where our support as fans also counts. Let's continue to cheer them on, regardless of the score. That's what being a strong team and a supportive community is all about.

Aisha: You're right, Sir. Let's keep cheering for them!

Rohan: (with determination) They can still win this!

Neha: (smiling optimistically) Let's not lose hope!

With renewed determination, the students resumed cheering for their school team, their voices echoing across the sports field. Harish Sir stood by them, proud of their resilience and spirit, knowing that win or lose, moments like these taught them invaluable lessons about teamwork, perseverance, and the unpredictable nature of life.

Multi-Thinking and the Art of Balance

It was a typical afternoon in Harish Sir's accountancy class. The students had just finished a challenging exercise on balance sheets and were now chatting among themselves, discussing how they balanced their studies with other aspects of their lives.

Rohan: (sighing) Man, that balance sheet exercise was tough. I barely managed to get everything to tally.

Aisha: I know, right? And with the football practice every evening, it's getting harder to keep up with all the homework.

Neha: (nodding) Yeah, I have dance classes three times a week, and it feels like there's no time left for anything else. Sometimes, I wonder how we're supposed to manage everything.

Rohan: (grinning) And then there are the weekends. My parents always have some family event or chores lined up. No time to relax or hang out with friends.

Aisha: (laughing) Tell me about it! Between school, extracurricular activities, and family stuff, it's like we're always multitasking. Do you guys ever get a moment to just breathe?

Neha: Rarely. But you know, it's kind of impressive how we manage to juggle everything. Sometimes I think we're like superheroes with all the multitasking we do.

Harish Sir: (noticing the conversation) You all seem to be handling a lot of things at once. Have you ever heard of multi-thinking?

The students looked at Harish Sir, curious about this new term.

Aisha: Multi-thinking? Is that like multitasking, Sir?

Harish Sir: Sort of, Aisha. You've all heard of multitasking, right? It's doing many things simultaneously with equal focus. People often say women are better at it than men, but regardless, young people like you are naturally great at it. You can listen to music, text a friend, chat on Skype, and message on Facebook, all while watching TV.

Rohan: Yeah, we do that all the time. But how is multi-thinking different, Sir?

Harish Sir: Good question, Rohan. Multi-thinking is about having more than one stream of thought running in your head constantly. For example, Krishna in the Bhagavad Gita tells Arjuna to think of God all the time, no matter what he's doing.

तस्मात्सर्वेषु कालेषु मामनुस्मर युध्य च ।
मय्यर्पितमनोबुद्धिर्मामेवैष्यस्यसंशयम् ॥

Therefore, always remember Me and also do your duty of fighting the war. With mind and intellect surrendered to Me, you will definitely attain Me; of this, there is no doubt.

This means keeping a positive, parallel thought alongside your main activity.

Neha: That sounds a bit complicated. Can we really think about something unrelated while focusing on our work?

Harish Sir: It might seem difficult, but it's quite natural. Think about the day before your final exams end and your summer vacation begins. Even while you're studying hard for your last exam, there's a happy thought-track running about the fun you'll have during the break. That's multi-thinking.

Aisha: Oh, I see! So, it's like having a positive thought alongside a stressful one?

Harish Sir: Exactly, Aisha. And it works for everything. Let's say you're playing a match and your main thought is, 'I have to win.' A parallel thought could be, 'I just need to play my best every minute.' This reduces pressure and keeps you focused on the effort, not just the result.

Rohan: And what about when we're studying a subject we don't like?

Harish Sir: If your main thought while doing homework is, 'I hate this subject,' your parallel thought could be, 'Every bit of this is making me smarter.' This positive track balances the negative one, making the process more bearable and even enjoyable.

Neha: What about when we have to do chores at home, Sir?

Harish Sir: Good example, Neha. If you're thinking, 'Why do I have to do this?' your parallel thought could be, 'This is a small way to help my family,' or 'I can get this done quickly and then enjoy my day.' This shift in perspective makes a big difference.

Aisha: So, it's all about practice, right?

Harish Sir: Yes, Aisha. Just like with any skill, practice is key. Regularly switching on your parallel thought-tracks will make them automatic. Eventually, your positive parallel track could become your main thought-track, bringing calm and contentment into your life. Krishna Says in verse 8 of chapter 8:

अभ्यासयोगयुक्तेन चेतसा नान्यगामिना ।
परमं पुरुषं दिव्यं याति पार्थानुचिन्तयन् ॥

With practice, O Parth, when you constantly engage the mind in remembering Me, the Supreme Divine Personality, without deviating, you will certainly attain Me.

Rohan: That sounds like a great thing to work towards, Sir.

Harish Sir: It definitely is, Rohan. Remember, practice makes perfect. Whether it's music, sports, or seeing the bright side of things, doing it over and over makes it second nature.

Harish Sir paused, letting the students absorb his words.

Harish Sir: The Gita says, "At all times, think of me and fight." This means keeping positive thoughts alongside your actions. Remember to thank the Universe for its gifts, see the big picture, and count your blessings.

With that, Harish Sir smiled at his students, who now looked more determined and inspired. They resumed their discussions with renewed energy, their spirits lifted by the powerful lesson they had just learned.

The Balance of the World: The Power of Right Actions

It was a gloomy afternoon, and the mood in Harish Sir's classroom matched the weather outside. The students had just returned from a particularly difficult week of exams and extracurricular activities, feeling worn out and disheartened. The room was filled with a sense of frustration and unfairness as the students began discussing their experiences.

Rohan: (sighing deeply) I don't get it, Sir. I study hard, help my friends with their homework, and try to be nice to everyone, but it feels like no one even notices. Meanwhile, there are people who barely put in any effort, but they're popular and seem to get everything they want.

Aisha: (nodding in agreement) It's so unfair. I try to do the right thing, but it feels like the people who lie and cheat always get ahead. They get the best opportunities and everyone loves them.

Neha: (frowning) And it's not just about recognition. Sometimes it feels like doing good just makes things harder. Why should we bother doing the right thing when it doesn't seem to make a difference?

Harish Sir: (listening attentively) I understand how you feel. It's tough to keep doing good when it seems like it doesn't pay off. But let me share a perspective from the Bhagavad Gita that might help us understand this better.

The students looked at Harish Sir with interest, hoping for some wisdom to help them make sense of their feelings.

Harish Sir: The Gita teaches us that no action is inherently good or evil. It's the intent behind the action that makes it so. Krishna explains to Arjuna that even a person with the vilest conduct can be considered righteous if they worship with undistracted devotion. This implies that what truly matters is our intention and devotion.

Rohan: But Sir, if that's the case, what's the point of trying to do good? Why not just do whatever we like and then pray for forgiveness?

Harish Sir: It's not quite that simple, Rohan. Hinduism places a great emphasis on the process of cause and effect. Every action we take sets off a chain of reactions that we can't always foresee or control. Right actions – those that are unselfish, responsible, and not driven by anger or greed – usually lead to good consequences. Wrong actions often lead to bad ones.

Aisha: But there are no guarantees, right? Even if we do the right thing, it can still lead to bad outcomes because of someone else's actions.

Harish Sir: Exactly, Aisha. There are no guarantees. Your right actions might lead to unintended consequences because of the actions of others. For example, imagine your uncle speeds through a red light to get you to a movie on time. Another car has to brake suddenly to avoid hitting your car, causing a biker to crash. You might get to the movie on time without any immediate consequences, but your uncle's wrong action has caused harm to someone else.

Neha: So, even right actions can lead to wrong consequences?

Harish Sir: Yes, Neha. That's the complexity of life. Sometimes it looks like those who do wrong get away with it, while those who do right suffer. But the reality is far more complex than we can see. We can't change the seemingly unfair events around us, but we can control our own actions and add to the balance of right actions in the world.

Rohan: But it still feels like there's no point if we can't see the results.

Harish Sir: Think of it this way, Rohan. The more people who perform right actions, the more the balance of the world tips towards goodness. Each of us contributes to this balance, and though we might not see the immediate effects, our actions matter in the grand scheme of things.

Rohan: Sir, could you explain that a bit more? And maybe give some examples?

Harish Sir: Certainly, Rohan. Let's take an example from a popular movie – the Joker from Batman. His actions were driven by what he perceived as the injustices and wrongs done to him by society. He believed he was simply responding to a world that treated him unfairly. However, if everyone acted based on revenge or negativity in response to their experiences, the world would indeed become a very chaotic and unhappy place.

Harish sir continued……………

This is where the ripple effect of actions comes into play. Just like positive actions can inspire and spread goodness, negative actions can do the opposite. The Joker's actions create a ripple of fear and chaos that affects everyone in Gotham. People become more distrustful, more fearful, and more inclined to act out of self-preservation rather than kindness or justice.

On the other hand, consider Batman. Despite facing his own tragedies and challenges, he chooses to fight for justice and protect the innocent. His actions are driven by a sense of duty and a desire to make the world a better place. Even though he faces setbacks and criticism, his positive actions inspire hope and courage in others.

Rohan: So, even if it feels like my good actions don't make a difference, they actually do?

Harish Sir: Absolutely, Rohan. Just as the Joker's negative actions had a widespread impact, your positive actions can create a ripple effect of goodness. By consistently performing right actions, you contribute to tipping the balance towards a better, more harmonious world. It's not about immediate recognition or reward, but about the long-term impact of our collective actions. Remember, the goal is to add to the fund of right actions and help create a world where goodness prevails over chaos and negativity.

Aisha: But what about the Gita's statement that no action is good or evil by itself? Most people would agree that killing someone is evil.

Harish Sir: It depends on the intent behind the action. If the action is unselfish and done out of a sense of duty, it's considered a right action. For example, a soldier fighting to protect his country or a hangman carrying out a lawful execution – their actions, though harsh, are driven by duty, not anger or greed.

Neha: But even if we act with the right intent, we might still face consequences, right?

Harish Sir: Yes, Neha. Suppose someone, like Dexter from the TV series, decides to kill a terrible person with the intent to stop further harm. If caught, society's laws will punish them. But according to the Gita, if the intent was pure and unselfish, they will find inner peace despite the punishment.

Rohan: That's a bit comforting, Sir. But what if we make mistakes and do wrong actions?

Harish Sir: The Gita teaches that even if we slip into wrong actions, there's always hope. If we truly repent and sincerely try to reform, we will be treated as righteous in the eyes of God and find inner peace and happiness.

Aisha: (smiling) That's a reassuring thought, Sir. It's like knowing there's always a chance for redemption.

Harish Sir: Exactly, Aisha. No matter how difficult things get, remember to keep your intentions pure and your actions righteous. That's the essence of the teachings in the Gita. "All he needs is love" And Harish Sir closed his eyes, smiled and recited a verse from Bhagwad Gita:

पत्रं पुष्पं फलं तोयं यो मे भक्त्या प्रयच्छति |
तदहं भक्त्युपहृतमश्नामि प्रयतात्मनः ||

Rohan: What does that mean, Sir?

Harish Sir: It means if one offers a leaf, a flower, a fruit, or a little water, with devotion and a heart that is pure, I will accept that gift of love. God does not need grand offerings. The simplest acts of devotion, done with pure intent, are what matter most.

Neha: (reflecting) So, it's really about the love and intent behind our actions.

Harish Sir: Exactly, Neha. All God needs is our love and devotion. No matter how small the offering, if it's given with a pure heart, it's enough.

The students sat quietly, absorbing Harish Sir's words. They felt a renewed sense of purpose and understanding, ready to face their challenges with a clearer perspective and a stronger commitment to doing the right thing.

Echoes of Intent: Navigating Life's Choices

Harish Sir looked around the classroom, his gaze settling on Rohan, Meera, Aisha, and Neha. They were huddled together in a corner, their heads bent over something that seemed to be causing a lot of excitement among them.

Curious, Harish Sir walked over and saw that they were planning a prank to play on another student, Varun, who had recently won a scholarship they all had their eyes on. Rohan was leading the discussion, suggesting ways to embarrass Varun in front of the whole school.

"What's going on here, Rohan?" Harish Sir asked, his voice calm but firm.

Rohan looked up, a mischievous grin on his face. "Sir, we were just thinking of teaching Varun a lesson. He always brags about his scholarship, and we thought it would be funny to—"

Harish Sir raised his hand to stop Rohan. "I understand what you're trying to do, but think carefully about your cause here. Is embarrassing Varun really the right thing to do?"

Meera spoke up, "But Sir, Varun is always boasting about how smart he is because he got that scholarship. It's not fair to the rest of us."

"Fairness is important, Meera," Harish Sir acknowledged. "But let's consider this: What if Varun's bragging is just a cover for his insecurities? What if he's trying to prove himself to his parents or to overcome some personal challenges?"

Aisha chimed in, "But Sir, shouldn't we stand up for ourselves? Varun shouldn't get away with making us feel less just because he got lucky with a scholarship."

Neha nodded in agreement. "Exactly, Sir. We're just trying to balance things out."

Harish Sir sat down beside them; his expression thoughtful. "I understand your feelings, but let me tell you a story from the Bhagavad Gita. Krishna teaches Arjuna about the importance of choosing our causes wisely. It's not just about standing up for ourselves or seeking revenge. It's about doing what is right and good, without causing harm to others."

He continued, "Think of it this way: Varun's success with the scholarship is like a rolling trophy. Today it's him, tomorrow it could be someone else. If you focus on bringing others down, you might succeed temporarily, but it won't bring you lasting happiness or fulfilment."

Rohan looked uncertain now. "But Sir, shouldn't we do something? Varun shouldn't get away with—"

Harish Sir interrupted gently, "Instead of focusing on bringing Varun down, why not focus on raising yourselves up? Use your energy and talents to achieve something positive for yourselves and others. Perhaps you could organize a study group to help each other with academics or start a community service project. That way, you're not just reacting to someone else's success but creating your own."

Meera sighed, starting to see Harish Sir's point. "So, it's not just about what we do, but why and how we do it?"

"Exactly," Harish Sir affirmed. "Choose causes that are unselfish, that uplift others and make a positive difference. That's where true success lies—not in tearing others down but in building yourself and your community up."

Harish Sir watched as Rohan, Meera, Aisha, and Neha settled back into their seats, deep in thought. Sensing their openness to learn more, he decided to share another perspective.

"You know," Harish Sir began, "there's a famous story about a student who was always jealous of his classmate's achievements. No matter how hard he tried, he couldn't surpass him. Frustrated, he spread rumours to tarnish his classmate's reputation."

Neha frowned, "Did it work?"

Harish Sir shook his head. "Initially, yes. His classmate faced difficulties, but eventually, the truth came out. The student who spread rumours was caught, and he faced severe consequences. His actions not only harmed his classmate but also damaged his own reputation."

Aisha leaned forward, "So, what should he have done instead?"

"He should have focused on improving himself," Harish Sir explained. "Like the champion swimmer who practices tirelessly to excel or the girl who wins dance competitions through dedication. They don't waste their energy on bringing others down. They focus on their goals with single-minded devotion."

Meera nodded thoughtfully. "I get it now. It's not just about what you achieve but how you achieve it."

"Exactly," Harish Sir agreed. "Krishna teaches in the Gita that success gained through unethical means doesn't last. It's like building a house on sand—it may stand for a while, but it will eventually collapse."

Rohan looked contemplative. "So, we should always think about the consequences of our actions?"

"Yes," Harish Sir affirmed. "Ask yourself: Is this cause benefiting others or just satisfying my ego? Are my actions based on jealousy or genuine concern for fairness and justice?"

He continued, "Imagine if everyone chose their causes wisely. Instead of tearing each other down, we'd build a supportive community where everyone thrives."

Neha sighed, "It's hard, though. Sometimes, it feels easier to retaliate than to take the higher road."

Harish Sir nodded sympathetically. "It is hard, but that's where true strength lies—in choosing the harder but right path. Remember, the rewards of working for a noble cause—self-confidence, inner peace—are invaluable and lasting."

Harish Sir continued, "Now, let's explore another aspect that Krishna teaches in the Gita. He reminds us that we humans have a tendency to categorize everything and everyone, putting them into neat little boxes based on superficial differences—skin colour, nationality, dietary habits, wealth, and even religious beliefs."

Rohan, intrigued, interjected, "But sir, why do we do that? Why do we need to categorize people?"

Harish Sir replied thoughtfully, "It's a way for us to feel in control, to create a sense of belonging by defining who is 'like us' and who is 'not like us'. However, this classification often leads to division, prejudice, and even conflict. We see wars between nations, hostility between different religious groups, and discrimination based on race or economic status."

Meera nodded in agreement, "It does seem absurd when you think about it. We create so much unnecessary tension and suffering by focusing on these differences."

Harish Sir continued, "Exactly. The Gita teaches us a profound truth—that God, in whatever form we choose to worship Him, whether as Ishvara, Allah, Jesus, Wahe Guru, or in any other form, doesn't concern Himself with these labels. What truly matters to Him is the purity of our hearts and the strength of our faith."

He recited a verse 21 of chapter 7 from Bhagwad Gita:

यो यो यां यां तनुं भक्त: श्रद्धयार्चितुमिच्छति | तस्य तस्याचलां श्रद्धां तामेव विदधाम्यहम् ||

Whatever may be the form a devotee seeks to worship with faith— in that form alone I make his faith unwavering.

Neha, reflecting on the idea, added, "So, it doesn't matter if we follow different traditions or beliefs, as long as we are sincere in our devotion?"

"Exactly, Neha," Harish Sir affirmed. "Krishna emphasizes that He accepts and blesses all sincere worship, regardless of its outward form. This inclusivity and acceptance are essential teachings that remind us to look beyond superficial differences and embrace the unity of all beings."

Aisha pondered for a moment before saying, "So, if we apply this to our lives, choosing a cause wisely means not just looking at the external rewards or appearances, but understanding the deeper impact of our actions and intentions."

Harish Sir smiled warmly, "You've grasped it perfectly, Aisha. When we choose our causes with unselfish motives, when our actions are guided by compassion and integrity, the rewards we gain—self-confidence, inner peace, and a sense of fulfilment—are far more enduring and valuable."

The students nodded, taking in the profound wisdom shared by their teacher. They understood that true success isn't just about achieving external goals but about nurturing a pure heart and steadfast faith in whatever cause they choose to devote themselves to.

Discovering Divinity within

Seated in a cozy corner of the bustling school cafeteria, bathed in the soft glow of morning sunlight filtering through the large windows, Rohan, Neha, Meera, and Aisha engaged in an animated discussion. Their recent exploration of the Bhagavad Gita had sparked a newfound interest in spiritual matters and the essence of existence.

Rohan, leaning in with enthusiasm, began the conversation.

Rohan: (gesturing animatedly) You know, guys, last night I was reading more about the Bhagavad Gita, and I stumbled upon this fascinating idea. It talks about how we are all connected to God, like we have a divine aspect within us.

Neha: (furrowing her brow thoughtfully) Hold on, Rohan. Isn't God supposed to be this all-powerful, omnipotent being? How can we be part of that?

Meera: (nodding in agreement) It does sound intriguing. I've heard snippets of this before, but I've never quite understood it fully.

Aisha: (leaning forward, curious) So, are we suggesting that each of us has a piece of God within us?

Their conversation paused momentarily as Harish Sir, their respected teacher and mentor, approached their table with a warm smile.

Harish Sir: (greeting them warmly) Good morning, everyone. I couldn't help but overhear your discussion. It seems like you're delving into some profound spiritual concepts this morning.

Rohan: (eagerly) Good morning, sir. Yes, we were just discussing this concept from the Gita about our connection to God within ourselves. Is that really possible?

Harish Sir: (taking a seat nearby) It's a question that has fascinated seekers of truth for centuries. The Bhagavad Gita teaches us about the divine essence that pervades all of existence, including our own beings.

Neha: (leaning in with curiosity) But sir, how can something as vast and transcendent as God be within us?

Harish Sir: (nodding thoughtfully) Think of it this way, Neha. Imagine a drop of water in the ocean—it's small compared to the vast ocean, yet it contains the essence of the entire ocean. Similarly, the Gita invites us to recognize the divine spark within us—the essence that connects us to the universal consciousness, often referred to as God.

Meera: (pondering) So, it's not about being miniature versions of God, but about realizing a deeper connection?

Harish Sir: (smiling warmly) Exactly, Meera. The Gita uses the analogy of the Knower of the field to illustrate this concept. It suggests that just as God comprehends all aspects of existence, the awareness of that divine presence resides within each of us as well. He explains to arjuna in verse 2 and 3 of chapter 13 of the Bhagwad Geeta.

इदं शरीरं कौन्तेय क्षेत्रमित्यभिधीयते |
क्षेत्रज्ञं चापि मां विद्धि सर्वक्षेत्रेषु भारत |
क्षेत्रक्षेत्रज्ञयोर्ज्ञानं यत्तज्ज्ञानं मतं मम ||
एतद्यो वेत्ति तं प्राहुः क्षेत्रज्ञ इति तद्विदः ||

O Arjun, this body is termed as kṣhetra (the field of activities), and the one who knows this body is called kṣhetrajña (the knower of the field) by the sages who discern the truth about both.

I am also the knower of all the individual fields of activity. The understanding of the body as the field of activities, and the soul and God as the knowers of the field, this I hold to be true knowledge.

Aisha: (thoughtfully) How can we experience this connection more tangibly, sir?

Harish Sir: (leaning forward) It begins with exploring our inner selves—not just our physical bodies, but our thoughts, emotions, and the deeper currents of consciousness. Through practices like meditation and self-reflection, we can start to glimpse this profound truth for ourselves.

Their conversation continued to unfold, guided by Harish Sir's wisdom and the students' growing curiosity. In the lively ambiance of the school cafeteria, amidst the clatter of trays and the hum of conversation, they embarked on a journey of discovery—a journey to uncover the divine within themselves and the world around them.

Their conversation continued to unfold, guided by Harish Sir's wisdom and the students' growing curiosity. In the lively ambiance of the school cafeteria, amidst the clatter of trays and the hum of conversation, they embarked on a journey of discovery—a journey to uncover the divine within themselves and the world around them.

Harish Sir, taking a moment to collect his thoughts, resumed the discussion with a gentle smile.

Harish Sir: You know, the concept of realizing our connection to God within us can be likened to stripping away the outer layers of something to understand its essence. Just like we discussed earlier about a light bulb and a treadmill, let's delve deeper into this idea.

Rohan: (nodding attentively) Yes, sir. You mentioned that if we strip away the physical aspects, we can see the essence that ties things together, like electricity in the case of a light bulb and a treadmill.

Harish Sir: (gesturing thoughtfully) Precisely. Imagine if we strip away everything that defines us physically—

our bodies, our thoughts, our senses—what remains? What's left is the essence, the life force that animates us. Similarly, if we strip away everything we perceive in the universe—the objects, the sounds, the tastes—what remains is the essence of the universe itself, the universal life force, often referred to as God.

Neha: (reflecting) So, in essence, the 'You Are God' statement means recognizing this universal life force within ourselves?

Harish Sir: (encouragingly) Absolutely, Neha. It's about understanding that the same life force that sustains the universe also sustains each of us. When we say 'Tat Tvam Asi'—You Are That—we acknowledge this fundamental unity between ourselves and the divine.

Meera: (intrigued) But sir, isn't God often described in terms of what He is not, rather than what He is?

Harish Sir: (nodding knowingly) Yes, Meera. Describing something as vast and ineffable as God can be challenging. The Vedic scholars used the technique of negation—Neti, Neti—to describe God. By stating what God is not—neither this, nor that—they guide us towards understanding that God transcends all definitions and limitations.

Aisha: (curiously) So, by eliminating what God is not, we come closer to understanding what God truly is?

Harish Sir: (smiling warmly) Exactly, Aisha. It's akin to peeling away layers of an onion. Each layer we remove brings us closer to the core essence. Similarly, every negation brings us closer to grasping the essence of God—the Supreme Soul, Brahman.

Their conversation flowed on, enriched by Harish Sir's patient explanations and the students' eagerness to explore profound truths. In the midst of their school cafeteria, where the aroma of freshly brewed coffee mingled with the voices of their peers, they embarked deeper into their journey of self-discovery and spiritual understanding.

In this lively exchange, amidst the clinking of cutlery and the murmur of fellow students, they unravelled timeless wisdom—the recognition that within each of them dwells a spark of the divine, awaiting discovery through introspection, contemplation, and a journey of the soul.

Garbage In, Garbage Out

In the serene hills of Dehradun, where the air was crisp with the scent of pine trees, Rohan, Neha, Meera, and Aisha found themselves engaged in a spirited debate over breakfast at their hotel. The annual school trip had brought them to this picturesque hill station, sparking discussions that ranged from the scenic beauty to deeper reflections on food and its impact on their lives.

Rohan: (with a thoughtful expression) You know, it's interesting how we're all enjoying the food here. We don't have fast food options like back home, but somehow, I'm not missing them.

Neha: (nodding in agreement) Yeah, I feel more satisfied with the meals here. They're simpler and seem healthier than the fast food we usually grab.

Meera: (curiously) I wonder if it's because we're surrounded by nature. The food feels more wholesome and fresher, doesn't it?

Their conversation paused briefly as Harish Sir joined them, having overheard their discussion.

Harish Sir: (smiling warmly) Good morning, everyone. Enjoying breakfast?

Rohan: (enthusiastically) Yes, sir! We were just discussing how the food here feels different from what we usually eat.

Harish Sir: (nodding thoughtfully) Food often tastes better when it's closer to its natural state and prepared with fresh ingredients. It's a noticeable difference, isn't it?

Frustration over Fast Food:

As they continued their conversation, some of the students' frustrations over the absence of fast-food options became evident.

Aisha: (frowning slightly) But sir, I really miss having burgers and fries. This trip would be perfect if we could just get some fast food once in a while.

Neha: (sympathetically) I get what you mean, Aisha. Sometimes, fast food just hits the spot, you know?

Rohan: (thoughtfully) Yeah, but isn't it strange how we crave fast food even when we're surrounded by such good food here?

Their discussion paused momentarily as Harish Sir listened intently, acknowledging their perspectives before offering his insights.

Harish Sir: (calmly) It's natural to crave convenience and familiar tastes, especially when we're used to certain foods. Fast food can be tempting, but it's important to consider how it affects our bodies and minds in the long run.

Aisha: (frustrated) But sir, why does something that tastes so good have to be so bad for us?

Harish Sir: (empathetically) Fast food often contains high levels of fats, sugars, and additives that can impact our health if consumed regularly. It's about finding a balance between enjoying what we like and making choices that support our well-being.

Exploring Different Perspectives:

Their debate expanded to include the broader implications of food choices, touching upon vegetarianism, non-vegetarian diets, and the benefits and drawbacks of each.

Meera: (inquiring) Sir, what about vegetarian versus non-vegetarian diets? I've heard arguments for both.

Harish Sir: (smiling warmly) That's a topic with varying perspectives indeed. Vegetarian diets have been extensively studied and often praised for their numerous health benefits and positive environmental impact. Research consistently shows that well-planned vegetarian diets tend to be lower in saturated fats and cholesterol, which can reduce the risk of heart disease and certain types of cancer. They are also typically higher in fibre, vitamins, and phytonutrients found in fruits, vegetables, nuts, and whole grains, promoting overall health and longevity.

Neha: (intrigued) So, vegetarian diets are not just about personal preference but have actual health benefits?

Harish Sir: (nodding) Absolutely, Neha. Plant-based diets are associated with lower rates of obesity, hypertension, and type 2 diabetes, making them a cornerstone of preventive health measures. From an environmental standpoint, vegetarian diets require fewer natural resources and produce lower greenhouse gas emissions compared to meat-based diets, contributing to sustainability and conservation efforts globally.

Meera: (reflectively) What about protein? I've heard concerns that vegetarian diets may not provide enough protein.

Harish Sir: (explaining patiently) It's a common misconception, Meera. While meat is a concentrated source of protein, plant-based sources like beans, lentils, tofu, nuts, and seeds are rich in protein too. Moreover, combining different plant-based foods throughout the day can easily meet our protein needs without the saturated fats and cholesterol found in meat. Athletes and active individuals worldwide increasingly adopt vegetarian or vegan diets to optimize performance and recovery while reducing their environmental footprint.

Rohan: (thoughtfully) So, choosing a vegetarian diet isn't just about personal health but also benefits the planet?

Harish Sir: (affirming) Absolutely, Rohan. By choosing vegetarian meals more often, we not only support our own health but also contribute to sustainable food systems and conservation efforts, ensuring a healthier planet for future generations.

Neha: (reflectively) So, it's not just about what we eat but also how it's prepared and its impact on our bodies and minds?

Harish Sir: (nodding) Absolutely, Neha. The quality and preparation of food play a crucial role in how we feel physically and emotionally.

As their breakfast progressed, Harish Sir encouraged them to delve deeper into the concept of 'You Are What You Consume', drawing from philosophical and practical perspectives.

Harish Sir: (leaning forward) Consider this: what we consume isn't just food. It includes everything that we take in—our thoughts, emotions, media we consume, and the environments we surround ourselves with. Just like food nourishes or harms our bodies, everything we consume impacts our minds and our lives.

Rohan: (thoughtfully) So, it's like the saying, 'Garbage in, garbage out'—what we put in influences what comes out?

Harish Sir: (smiling) Exactly, Rohan. Whether it's food, information, or experiences, what we consume shapes our health, our perspectives, and even our actions.

Meera: (curiously) Sir, how can we apply this idea practically in our lives?

Harish Sir: (reflectively) Start by being mindful of what you choose to consume. Opt for foods that nourish your body, thoughts that uplift your spirit, and environments that support your well-being. It's about finding a balance that promotes physical, mental, and emotional health. Just like with food, there is good information you can consume - nourishing books, uplifting music, inspiring television programmes, and so on; there is stuff that is neither too bad nor too good; and there is absolute junk. Whether you like it or not, what you consume affects your mind, your mood and your actions.

Aisha: (curiously) Sir, you mostly advocate vegetarian food. Apart from health benefits and environmental impact, is there any spiritual connection as well?

Harish Sir: (smiling thoughtfully) Indeed, Aisha. Many spiritual traditions across the world promote vegetarianism as a means to cultivate compassion and respect for all living beings. It aligns with the principle of ahimsa, or non-violence, which is central to various philosophies and religions. Eating vegetarian is seen as a way to foster a deeper connection with nature and promote harmony within oneself and with others. It's not just about what we eat but also how our choices reflect our values and beliefs.

Neha: (nodding in understanding) That makes sense, sir. It's about considering the broader impact of our food choices on our health, the environment, and our spiritual well-being.

Harish Sir: Absolutely, Neha. Whether for health, environmental, or spiritual reasons, choosing a vegetarian diet is a mindful decision that can lead to personal and planetary wellness. It's about nourishing ourselves and our world in ways that resonate with our values and contribute to a better future for all.

Aisha: (nodding thoughtfully) So, it's not just about avoiding junk food; it's about choosing everything we consume wisely.

Rohan: (still curious) So, what should we eat to stay healthy, especially on a trip like this?

Harish Sir: (smiling) That's a good question, Rohan. A healthy diet should include a variety of foods that provide all the necessary nutrients our bodies need to function properly.

Neha: (intrigued) Can you give us some examples, sir?

Harish Sir: (smiling) Sure. In Ayurveda, the traditional Indian system of medicine, a balanced diet is essential for maintaining health. According to Ayurveda, a Sattvik diet is considered to be the most beneficial for the mind and body. This diet includes:

1) Fruits of all types, especially those that are naturally sweet.

2) All vegetables, except onion and garlic.

3) Whole grains like barley, wheat, and rice.

4) Beans like rajma and chana, dals.

5) Plant-based oils, like sunflower, groundnut, and olive oil.

6) Nuts and seeds, especially almonds that have been soaked in water and peeled.

7) Natural raw sugar, molasses, honey (in a glass of warm water with the juice of half a lemon squeezed into it).

8) Milk, butter, curd, cottage cheese.

9) Sweet spices, like cinnamon, cardamom, mint, basil, turmeric, ginger, cumin, and fennel.

10) Food prepared with love, for which you thank the Universe before eating.

Rohan: (surprised) That sounds pretty comprehensive.

Harish Sir: (smiling) Yes, it is. Foods that bestow long life, a stable mind, strength, health, happiness, and joy are much loved by the 'good' people, the Sattviks. Ayurveda believes that treatment for any condition should treat not just the condition but the entire body and mind. This is why a typical Ayurvedic treatment will involve yoga for physical fitness, meditation, and breathing exercises to calm the mind, massages for physical well-being, a strict diet consisting of easy-to-digest 'Sattvik' food, and finally, medication.

Neha: (reflecting) So, it's not just about avoiding junk food but about making mindful choices that nourish our body, mind, and spirit?

Harish Sir: (affirming) Exactly, Neha. Remember, a healthy mind in a healthy body is essential for overall well-being.

Harish Sir: (quoting verse 8 of chapter 17 of Bhagwad Gita)

आयुःसत्त्वबलारोग्यसुखप्रीतिविवर्धनाः |
रस्याः स्निग्धाः स्थिरा हृद्या आहाराः सात्त्विकप्रियाः ||

Persons in the mode of goodness prefer foods that promote life span, and increase virtue, strength, health, happiness, and satisfaction. Such foods are juicy, succulent, nourishing, and naturally tasteful.

So, by being mindful of what we eat and consume, we can ensure that we are in the pink of physical, mental, emotional, and spiritual health always. Think it's worth a try?

Students: (nodding and smiling) Yes, sir!

The students continued their meal with a newfound appreciation for the simple, nutritious food they were enjoying, understanding the deeper connections between their choices and overall well-being.

Finding the perfect blend of the Gunas (Qualities)

The crisp night air in Dehradun was filled with excitement as the students gathered for their stargazing activity. The trip had been packed with adventure and learning, but tonight promised something different – a chance to connect with the vast universe above.

As the students lay on their backs on a blanket spread over the grass, the only sound was the occasional rustling of leaves and the soft murmur of the forest. The sky was clear, and the stars were scattered like glittering jewels, twinkling and winking at the earth below. A sense of peace enveloped them, and in the stillness of the night, the students began to feel a deep inner calm.

Rohan: (whispering) This is amazing. Look at all those stars! It makes you feel so small, doesn't it?

Aisha: (nodding) Yeah, it's like we're just a tiny part of something so much bigger. It's beautiful.

Meera: (thoughtfully) It's moments like these that make me think about nature – not just the stars, but everything around us. Every part of nature has its own beauty and purpose.

Neha: (agreeing) True. And it's interesting how people are like that too. We're all so different, yet we all have our own roles to play.

Harish Sir: (smiling, joining the conversation) You've touched on something very profound, Neha. Just like nature, human beings too have different qualities and characteristics that make us unique.

Aisha: (curious) What do you mean, sir?

Harish Sir: (explaining) Hindus believe that everything in nature, including human beings, is influenced by three fundamental qualities or states of being, known as Gunas. These are Sattva, Rajas, and Tamas. These Gunas are constantly in flux and determine our thoughts, actions, and behaviors. Krishna describes this in Bhagwad Gita in verse 5 of chapter 14:

सत्त्वं रजस्तम इति गुणाः प्रकृतिसम्भवाः |
निबध्नन्ति महाबाहो देहे देहिनमव्ययम् ||

Material nature consists of three modes – goodness, passion and ignorance. When the eternal living entity comes in contact with nature, O mighty-armed Arjuna, he becomes conditioned by these modes.

Rohan: (intrigued) Can you tell us more about these Gunas, sir?

Harish Sir: (nodding) Of course, Rohan. Let's start with Sattva. Sattva is associated with purity, harmony, and balance. When Sattva is dominant in a person, they feel peaceful, clear-headed, and content. They enjoy activities that bring them joy and knowledge and often prefer solitude or the company of like-minded individuals. Bhagwad Gita verse 6 chapter 14:

तत्र सत्त्वं निर्मलत्वात्प्रकाशकमनामयम् |
सुखसङ्गेन बध्नाति ज्ञानसङ्गेन चानघ ||

O sinless one, the mode of goodness, being purer than the others, is illuminating, and it frees one from all sinful reactions. Those situated in that mode become conditioned by a sense of happiness and knowledge.

Neha: (reflecting) So, people with more Sattva are generally calm and positive?

Harish Sir: (affirming) Yes, Neha. But it's important to maintain a balance. Too much Sattva can make one complacent or detached from necessary actions.

Meera: (interested) What about the other Gunas?

Harish Sir: (continuing) Rajas is the quality of activity, energy, and passion. When Rajas is dominant, people feel motivated, driven, and ambitious. They are the ones who set goals and work tirelessly to achieve them. However, excessive Rajas can lead to stress, aggression, and restlessness. Bhagwad Gita verse 7 chapter 14:

रजो रागात्मकं विद्धि तृष्णासङ्गसमुद्भवम् |
तन्निबध्नाति कौन्तेय कर्मसङ्गेन देहिनम् ||

The mode of passion is born of unlimited desires and longings, O son of Kuntī, and because of this the embodied living entity is bound to material fruitive actions.

Aisha: (thoughtful) So, Rajas can be both good and bad, depending on the balance?

Harish Sir: (nodding) Exactly, Aisha. It provides the drive to accomplish things but must be tempered with calmness to avoid burnout. The third Guna is Tamas, which represents inertia, darkness, and ignorance. When Tamas is dominant, people feel lazy, confused, and lethargic. While some Tamas is necessary for rest and recovery, too much can lead to stagnation and depression. Bhagwad Gita verse 7 chapter 14

तमस्त्वज्ञानजं विद्धि मोहनं सर्वदेहिनाम् |
प्रमादालस्यनिद्राभिस्तन्निबध्नाति भारत ||

O son of Bharata, know that the mode of darkness, born of ignorance, is the delusion of all embodied living entities. The results of this mode are madness, indolence and sleep, which bind the conditioned soul.

Rohan: (curiously) So, do these Gunas change all the time?

Harish Sir: (smiling) Yes, they do, Rohan. Our state of mind fluctuates based on these Gunas throughout the day. For instance, after a good night's sleep, you might feel Sattvik – calm and clear-headed. During the day, as you engage in various activities, Rajas might dominate, making you energetic and active. If you overexert yourself, you might feel Tamasik, leading to tiredness and lethargy.

Neha: (pondering) That makes sense. I've noticed that I feel different at different times of the day.

Harish Sir: (encouraging) Exactly, Neha. It's about recognizing these states and striving to maintain a balance. The goal is to cultivate more Sattva, leading to a balanced and harmonious life.

Meera: (inquiring) How can we increase Sattva in our lives, sir?

Harish Sir: (smiling) Great question, Meera. Simple practices like meditation, mindful eating, and spending time in nature can help. Engaging in activities that bring joy and knowledge, and surrounding yourself with positive influences, can also enhance Sattva.

प्रकाशं च प्रवृत्तिं च मोहमेव च पाण्डव |
न द्वेष्टि सम्प्रवृत्तानि न निवृत्तानि काङ् क्षति ||
उदासीनवदासीनो गुणैर्यो न विचाल्यते |
गुणा वर्तन्त इत्येवं योऽवतिष्ठति नेङ्गते ||

The Supreme Divine Personality said: O Arjun, the persons who are transcendental to the three guṇas neither hate illumination (which is born of sattva), nor activity (which is born of rajas), nor even delusion (which is born of tamas), when these are abundantly present, nor do they long for them when they are absent. They remain neutral to the modes of nature and are not disturbed by them. Knowing it is only the guṇas that act, they stay established in the self, without wavering.

Aisha: (reflecting) It sounds like a balanced approach to living.

Harish Sir: (nodding) Yes, Aisha. A balanced approach helps us navigate through life's challenges more effectively. Remember, your better nature is always within you. By becoming best friends with it, you can avoid being stuck in negative states and lead a fulfilling life.

Rohan: (curiously) So, these Gunas are like the seasons we experience?

Harish Sir: (smiling) That's a wonderful analogy, Rohan. Just as nature goes through cycles of creation, preservation, and destruction, we too experience these cycles within ourselves. Spring represents Sattva – the season of new beginnings and harmony. Summer represents Rajas – the season of activity and growth. Autumn and winter represent Tamas – the seasons of rest and dormancy.

Neha: (thoughtfully) It's fascinating how everything is interconnected.

Harish Sir: (agreeing) Indeed, Neha. Understanding these connections helps us appreciate the diversity in nature and in ourselves. It reminds us that every aspect of our personality has a purpose and contributes to our overall growth.

Aisha: (pondering) So, it's about embracing our unique nature and finding harmony within ourselves?

Harish Sir: (smiling warmly) Precisely, Aisha. Embrace your uniqueness, strive for balance, and recognize that each Guna has its role. By doing so, you cultivate a better version of yourself.

Rohan: (excited) This is so interesting, sir! I feel like I've learned so much tonight.

Harish Sir: (pleased) I'm glad to hear that, Rohan. Remember, the journey to understanding ourselves is continuous. Keep exploring, keep learning, and always strive for balance.

Neha: (smiling) Thank you, sir. This has been an enlightening discussion.

Harish Sir: (smiling back) You're welcome, Neha. Let's take a moment to appreciate the silence and the stars, and reflect on what we've learned tonight.

The students lay back, feeling a deep sense of inner peace as they gazed at the stars. The conversation had not only deepened their understanding of the world around them but also of their own inner nature. The night sky, vast and infinite, seemed to mirror the limitless potential within each of them.

In the stillness of the night, the students absorbed the wisdom of the ancient teachings, feeling a sense of connection to the universe and a newfound clarity within themselves.

Be a God/Good Person

It was a sunny afternoon at the bustling Madhav International School. The students were busy with their various activities, eagerly discussing their upcoming exams and planning their weekend outings. Among them was Neha, a bright and ambitious student who had recently been feeling overwhelmed and anxious.

Neha had been struggling with the pressure to fit in with her peers. In her quest to be popular, she had made some questionable choices, including skipping classes and lying to her parents about her grades. The guilt and stress were weighing heavily on her mind.

During lunch, Neha found herself sitting alone in the school courtyard, lost in her thoughts. She had been pushing herself to excel in her studies, participate in extracurricular activities, and maintain her social life. But no matter how hard she tried; she couldn't escape the pressure she felt to be perfect in every aspect of her life.

Mr. Harish, who was passing by, noticed Neha's distress and decided to sit down beside her. "Neha, you seem troubled. What's on your mind?" he asked gently.

Neha looked up; her eyes filled with worry. "Sir, I've made some mistakes. I've lied and done things I'm not proud of, just to fit in. And now, I'm scared. I don't pray or worship God like some of my friends do. Does that make me a bad person? Am I not one of His children because of that?"

Mr. Harish smiled reassuringly. "Neha, that's a very important question. Let's talk about it. Do you think someone who doesn't worship God can still be a good person?"

Neha hesitated, then shrugged. "I don't know, Sir. My parents say that faith is important, but I see good people who don't necessarily pray or go to temples."

Mr. Harish nodded. "This is a great point, and it reminds me of a profound lesson from the Bhagavad Gita. Despite being a religious scripture, the Gita teaches that devotion to God is not a prerequisite for being a good person."

Neha listened intently as Mr. Harish continued, "In one of the chapters, Krishna, who has just revealed himself as the Lord Incarnate, lists qualities that make a person dear to God. Interestingly, none of these qualities require worshipping God. What matters more is how you live your life and treat others."

Neha's eyes widened in surprise. "Really? What qualities are those?"

Harish Sir received the verse from chapter 12 of Bhagwad Gita:

सन्तुष्ट: सततं योगी यतात्मा दृढनिश्चय: |
मय्यर्पितमनोबुद्धियों मद्भक्त: स मे प्रिय: ||

He by whom no one is put into difficulty and who is not disturbed by anyone, who is equipoised in happiness and distress, fear and anxiety, is very dear to Me.

यस्मान्नोद्विजते लोको लोकान्नोद्विजते च य: |
हर्षामर्षभयोद्वेगैर्मुक्तो य: स च मे प्रिय: ||

My devotee who is not dependent on the ordinary course of activities, who is pure, expert, without cares, free from all pains, and not striving for some result, is very dear to Me.

सम: शत्रौ च मित्रे च तथा मानापमानयो: |
शीतोष्णसुखदु:खेषु सम: सङ्गविवर्जित: ||
तुल्यनिन्दास्तुतिर्मौनी सन्तुष्टो येन केनचित् |
अनिकेत: स्थिरमतिर्भक्तिमान्मे प्रियो नर: ||

One who is equal to friends and enemies, who is equipoised in honour and dishonour, heat and cold, happiness and distress, fame and infamy, who is always free from contaminating association, always silent and satisfied with anything, who doesn't care for any residence, who is fixed in knowledge and who is engaged in devotional service – such a person is very dear to Me.

Mr. Harish explained, "Krishna mentions qualities like honesty, compassion, humility, and self-control. These are universal values that anyone can cultivate, regardless of their faith or belief in a higher power."

He added, "Think about why not having these qualities might make you unhappy or anxious. For instance, lying can lead to guilt, and anger can cloud your judgment. These negative emotions can destroy your peace of mind and sense of contentment."

Neha reflected on this. "So, it's more about being a good person through our actions and intentions?"

"Exactly," Mr. Harish replied. "You don't need to worship God to be a good person. What matters is embodying these universal values that bring peace and contentment, both to yourself and to those around you."

Neha felt a sense of relief wash over her. "Thank you, Sir. I think I understand now."

Mr. Harish smiled. "Remember, Neha, true goodness transcends religious boundaries. It's about how you live your life and the positive impact you have on others. You are not defined by your mistakes but by your efforts to be better every day."

Aisha pondered this for a moment. "So, you're saying that it's more important to focus on being a good person and finding contentment within myself than trying to be perfect in everything?"

"Exactly," Harish Sir replied. "Let's take this as an intellectual exercise. Why don't we go through some of the qualities Krishna mentioned and think about why lacking them could make us unhappy or anxious?"

Aisha nodded eagerly. "Okay, that sounds like a good idea."

Harish Sir started, "Let's start with kindness. Imagine if you were always harsh and unkind to others. How do you think that would affect your peace of mind?"

Aisha thought for a moment. "I guess being unkind would make me feel guilty and isolated. It would definitely create tension in my relationships."

"Exactly," Harish Sir said. "Now, think about equanimity - treating blame and praise with the same attitude. If you were always chasing praise and fearing blame, how would that impact you?"

"I would be constantly anxious and dependent on others' opinions for my happiness," Aisha replied.

Harish Sir nodded. "Yes, and finally, self-sufficiency. If you always depended on others for your happiness and blamed them for your unhappiness, how would that make you feel?"

"I would feel powerless and frustrated because I wouldn't be in control of my own happiness," Aisha said thoughtfully.

"Exactly," Harish Sir agreed. "By cultivating these qualities, you can find a sense of peace and contentment that no external achievement can provide."

Aisha smiled, feeling a weight lift off her shoulders. "Thank you, Harish Sir. This has been really enlightening. I think I understand now that true happiness comes from within and from being a good person."

Harish Sir smiled back. "I'm glad to hear that, Aisha. Remember, it's not about being perfect. It's about being kind, balanced, and self-sufficient. That's the true path to peace and contentment."

As they finished their conversation, Aisha felt a renewed sense of clarity and purpose. She realized that by focusing on these qualities, she could find the inner peace she had been searching for, and that would ultimately lead her to true success and happiness. Neha stood up, ready to face her challenges with a better understanding of what it means to be a good person. The lesson she learned that day stayed with her, guiding her towards a path of genuine self-improvement and inner peace.

Rediscovering Identity: Beyond Caste and Labels

It was a sunny afternoon at the bustling day in the school. The students were engaged in various activities, eagerly discussing their upcoming exams and planning their weekend outings. Among them was Meera, a curious and thoughtful student who loved delving into discussions about history and society.

One day, during lunch, Meera and her friends, Rohan, Aisha, and Neha, found themselves in a lively conversation about past traditions and how they shape the present. The discussion naturally drifted towards the Indian caste system, which they had recently studied in their history class.

"Why is there so much discrimination in our society based on caste?" Meera asked, her voice filled with curiosity and concern. "It's supposed to be about our nature and profession, not something we're born into."

Rohan, munching on his sandwich, nodded. "Yeah, it doesn't make sense. Originally, the caste system was meant to classify people by their professions: Brahmins were the intellectuals, Kshatriyas were the warriors, Vaishyas were the traders, and Shudras were the manual labourers. But now, it seems like people are judged by their birth, not their abilities."

Aisha chimed in, "And it's really affecting us. Some of my friends are treated differently just because of their last names. It's unfair."

Just then, Mr. Harish, their favourite teacher, walked by and overheard their conversation. He decided to join them, sensing an opportunity to share some valuable insights. "I see you're having a deep discussion about the caste system," he remarked, taking a seat. "Would you like to hear what the Bhagavad Gita has to say about this?"

The students eagerly nodded, and Mr. Harish began. "The Gita offers a profound perspective on caste. Krishna explains that it's not your parents, or your work, that defines you. Your nature does."

He continued, "Originally, the caste system was a way to classify people according to their professions: Brahmins were priests and teachers, Kshatriyas were warriors and rulers, Vaishyas were merchants, and Shudras were workers. Each caste was considered equally important to society. They were like different parts of the body: the head, the arms, the stomach, and the legs. No part is superior or inferior; all are essential for the body to function."

"But over time," Mr. Harish said, "the system got distorted. Caste became linked to birth rather than profession, leading to discrimination. People began to believe that some castes were superior to others, which is not what the original system intended."

Meera, intrigued, asked, "So what does the Gita say about this?"

"Krishna offers an alternative view," Mr. Harish explained. "he says it's neither a person's profession nor birth that makes them a Brahmin, Kshatriya, Vaishya, or Shudra, but their nature. For example, high-thinking individuals who are calm, tolerant, and disciplined are Brahmins by nature. It's about the qualities you embody, not your lineage."

He added, "Take historical figures like saint Tukaram, who was a farmer, or Valmiki, the author of the Ramayana, who was a reformed bandit. They are revered not because of their birth but because of their nature and deeds. Mahatma Gandhi, born into a Vaishya family, displayed both Brahmin and Kshatriya qualities."

Rohan asked, "What about people who are leaders or entrepreneurs? How do they fit into this?"

"Good question," Mr. Harish said. "People who lead and fight for justice, like activists or heroes, are Kshatriyas by nature. Entrepreneurs and those who generate wealth are Vaishyas. And those who prefer to follow instructions and do a good job in their tasks are Shudras. Each role is valuable and necessary."

He looked at the students, seeing their minds processing this new understanding. "The Gita teaches that happiness comes from staying true to your nature. If you act according to your true self, you'll find contentment. But if you try to be someone you're not, you'll only face frustration."

To illustrate, Mr. Harish gave an example, "Imagine you run for House Captain because you think it's cool, but your true passion is reading quietly in the library. If elected, you might end up hating the responsibilities and neglecting your duties, leading to unhappiness for you and others. It's a lose-lose situation."

The students sat in thoughtful silence, absorbing the wisdom of Mr. Harish's words. They realized that their true value lay not in societal labels or religious practices but in their nature and actions. With this newfound understanding, they felt a sense of liberation, ready to embrace their true selves and respect others for who they truly were.

Breaking the silence, Mr. Harish added, "There's another important lesson from the Gita that ties into this. Before jumping into something, think about why you are doing it. When you feel bad that you did not get something you really wanted, ask yourself why you wanted it so badly, and whether the fact that you did not get it was actually a good thing. The answers will help you decide whether or not you should continue with your action, or whether or not you should continue to feel bad."

Seeing puzzled looks on their faces, he elaborated with an example. "Let's say, for instance, you aspire to be the school's debate champion because you think it would make you popular. However, your true passion lies in painting, which brings you peace and joy. If you fail to win the debate competition, you'll feel disheartened. But if you reflect on why, you wanted it in the first place— was it for genuine interest in debating or just for popularity? —you might realize that not winning the debate could actually be a good thing. It frees up your time to focus on painting, where your true happiness lies."

Rohan, looking thoughtful, said, "So, it's about being honest with ourselves, right?"

"Exactly," Mr. Harish confirmed. "If you are honest with yourself, you may often be surprised at your answers. This self-reflection helps you align your actions with your true nature, leading to greater satisfaction and less inner conflict. Go on, try it and see!"

Aisha pondered aloud, "I guess sometimes we get so caught up in trying to meet others' expectations or chasing things we think we should want that we lose sight of what truly makes us happy."

"That's very insightful, Aisha," Mr. Harish said, encouragingly. "Staying true to your nature will guide you toward a more fulfilling life. Remember, the Gita teaches us the same where Krishna says in verse 47 of chapter 18

श्रेयान्स्वधर्मो विगुण: परधर्मात्स्वनुष्ठितात् |
स्वभावनियतं कर्म कुर्वन्नाप्नोति किल्बिषम् ||

It is better to engage in one's own occupation(dharma), even though one may perform it imperfectly, than to accept another's occupation and perform it perfectly. Duties prescribed according to one's nature are never affected by sinful reactions.

So, following your own path, aligned with your inherent nature, brings the most progress and happiness."

As the lunch bell rang, signalling the end of their break, the students felt enlightened and motivated. The conversation with Mr. Harish had given them a new perspective on the caste system and a deeper understanding of how to navigate their own lives with integrity and self-awareness.

Walking back to their classes, Meera, Rohan, Aisha, and Neha felt a sense of clarity. They were determined to apply these lessons in their lives, understanding that their true worth lay not in societal labels or external achievements but in their own unique nature and the virtues they cultivated within themselves.

Discovering Wisdom: The Relevance of the Bhagavad Gita

Throughout our journey exploring various chapters inspired by the teachings of the Bhagavad Gita, we have delved into profound concepts that resonate deeply with our lives as students and young individuals navigating the complexities of today's world. From understanding the essence of spirituality to grappling with the realities of human desires and the nature of happiness, each chapter has offered us valuable insights and perspectives.

In the first chapter, we explored the fundamental teachings of the Gita on spirituality and the pursuit of knowledge. We learned that spirituality isn't confined to religious rituals but encompasses a deeper understanding of ourselves and our place in the universe. This foundational wisdom encourages us to seek clarity and purpose in our lives, transcending superficial pursuits.

Moving forward, we examined the intricacies of human desires and the cycle of pleasure and pain. Through the lens of the Gita, we understood that while desires are natural, unchecked desires lead to suffering and discontent. This awareness empowers us to cultivate mindfulness and discernment in our choices, fostering a balanced approach to life's challenges.

In subsequent chapters, we explored the themes of karma and duty, learning that our actions shape our destiny and contribute to the greater good of society. The Gita's emphasis on fulfilling our responsibilities with sincerity and integrity resonates deeply with our roles as students, encouraging us to strive for excellence while upholding moral values. The discussions on caste and identity offered us a critical reflection on societal norms and prejudices. We discovered that true merit lies not in birth or social status but in our inherent qualities and actions. This insight challenges us to confront biases and strive for a more inclusive and just society where individuals are valued for their character and contributions.

Lastly, we contemplated the importance of self-awareness and authenticity in pursuing happiness. The Gita teaches us that true fulfilment comes from aligning our actions with our inner nature and values. By embracing our strengths and passions, we empower ourselves to lead purposeful lives driven by inner peace and contentment.

In conclusion, the Bhagavad Gita serves as a timeless guidebook for navigating life's complexities with wisdom and grace. Its teachings transcend religious boundaries, offering universal truths that are relevant to people of all ages and backgrounds. As students, understanding the Gita equips us with invaluable tools for personal growth, ethical decision-making, and compassionate leadership.

Therefore, each and every student should endeavour to understand the Bhagavad Gita not only for its philosophical richness but also for its practical applications in daily life. By integrating its teachings into our thoughts and actions, we can cultivate resilience, empathy, and a deeper sense of purpose. Let us embark on this journey of self-discovery and spiritual awakening, drawing inspiration from the timeless wisdom of the Bhagavad Gita to create a brighter and more harmonious future for ourselves and our communities.

Final Words:
Guiding Youth Toward Wisdom and Purpose

Dear Student's,

As we come to the end of this journey exploring spirituality together, I'm reminded of a story about a young student named Arjun. Arjun was ambitious and driven, always striving to excel in academics and sports. But despite his achievements, he often felt a sense of emptiness and confusion about his future.

One day, Arjun met an elderly neighbour, Mr. Sharma, who was known for his calm demeanour and insightful advice. Curious about Mr. Sharma's peaceful outlook, Arjun asked him, "How do you stay so calm and happy all the time?"

Mr. Sharma smiled and invited Arjun to his garden. He pointed to a small plant struggling to grow amidst the weeds. "You see this plant, Arjun? It's like our mind. Sometimes, it's crowded with doubts and fears, much like these weeds. But just as I tend to this garden, we can nurture our minds."

He handed Arjun a watering can and said, "Water it with positive thoughts, patience, and gratitude. Watch how it flourishes." As Arjun watered the plant, Mr. Sharma continued, "Spirituality is like nurturing this garden within us. It's about finding peace amid life's challenges and understanding our true purpose."

Arjun realized that his journey wasn't just about achievements but also about inner growth and happiness. Inspired by Mr. Sharma's wisdom, he started practicing mindfulness and gratitude daily. Over time, Arjun felt more at peace with himself and more connected to others.

Dear friends, like Arjun, each of us navigates our own path through life's ups and downs. Through this journey together, we've explored how spirituality offers us tools to find meaning, resilience, and inner peace.

In these pages, we have touched upon timeless truths and practical wisdom that resonate across cultures and generations. We have learned that spirituality is not confined to temples or scriptures alone but permeates every facet of existence—our thoughts, actions, and relationships.

At its heart, spirituality is an invitation—an invitation to delve deeper into the mystery of life, to embrace the unknown with humility and grace. It calls us to cultivate inner stillness amidst life's turbulence, to find solace in the silence of our hearts, and to recognize the interconnectedness of all beings.

Throughout this book, we have witnessed the transformative power of spiritual practices—meditation that calms the restless mind, acts of kindness that awaken compassion, and moments of contemplation that unveil profound insights. These practices are not mere rituals but gateways to awakening, guiding us towards a life of purpose, meaning, and fulfilment.

Rohan's Transformation: Rohan's journey through adversity led him to discover profound transformation through spirituality. From a vibrant teenager weighed down by academic pressures, social expectations, and personal setbacks, he found solace and guidance in the teachings of the Bhagavad Gita and the support of his grandmother. Through meditation, yoga, and a deepening understanding of inner peace, Rohan not only healed but also grew stronger spiritually. His story highlights the importance of resilience, self-discovery, and finding meaning beyond material success. It serves as a reminder that amidst life's challenges, there exists a path to personal growth and fulfilment through spiritual practices and self-awareness.

Neha's Path to Healing: Neha, known for her vibrant spirit and infectious laughter, navigated high school with boundless energy and a penchant for leadership. Her charisma drew peers to her, yet amidst successes like the debate competition, tensions arose with Riya due to perceived competitiveness. Misunderstandings spread, leading to Neha's isolation and academic decline. Discovering solace under a banyan tree with Priyanshi, Neha embarked on a spiritual journey. Through meditation and teachings from the Bhagavad Gita, she found clarity and reconciled with her past actions. Apologizing to friends, she rebuilt relationships and regained academic focus, guided by newfound wisdom and inner peace.

Raj's Enlightenment: The story of Raj illustrates that true transformation begins with self-awareness and guidance. Through mentorship and spiritual teachings, Raj learns to channel his charisma and energy positively, overcoming challenges such as academic apathy and impulsive behaviour. His journey highlights the importance of self-reflection, resilience, and the power of guidance in navigating the complexities of adolescence.

Raj's story emphasizes that with the right mindset and support, anyone can overcome challenges, find inner peace, and lead a purposeful life.

These narratives collectively underscore several universal insights about spirituality. They highlight that spiritual growth is not confined to any particular religion or belief system but is a universal path accessible to all seekers, regardless of their backgrounds or circumstances. Through personal stories, we witness the transformative power of spiritual practices such as meditation, mindfulness, and community engagement in cultivating resilience, finding purpose, and fostering inner peace.

From the timeless wisdom embedded in ancient texts to the personal journeys of modern seekers, the path of spiritual growth unfolds as a profound and continuous evolution. It encompasses various dimensions that enrich our understanding of self and the world around us:

Self-Discovery: At the heart of spiritual growth lies the journey of self-discovery. Through practices of introspection, meditation, and mindfulness, we embark on a quest to unravel the layers of our identity. We delve deep into the recesses of our psyche, confronting both the light and shadow aspects of our being. This inner exploration leads us to discern our authentic selves beyond societal roles, conditioned beliefs, and external expectations. As we cultivate self-awareness, we gain clarity on our values, passions, and purpose in life. Each moment of introspection becomes a revelation, guiding us towards a deeper understanding of our innate strengths and vulnerabilities.

Resilience: Spiritual teachings serve as a guiding light during life's inevitable trials and tribulations. They impart timeless principles that nurture resilience and fortitude in the face of adversity. Through spiritual growth, we learn to embrace challenges not as obstacles but as opportunities for personal and spiritual evolution. We recognize that setbacks and hardships are integral parts of the human experience, offering profound lessons and insights that propel us forward on our path. With a resilient spirit, we navigate storms with grace, harnessing inner strength and faith to endure, adapt, and grow amidst life's ebb and flow.

Compassion: Central to spiritual growth is the cultivation of compassion—both towards ourselves and others. As we deepen our spiritual practice, we awaken to the interconnectedness of all beings and the shared human experience. Compassion emerges as a natural outpouring of this awareness, fostering empathy, kindness, and understanding in our interactions. We learn to embrace our imperfections and vulnerabilities with self-compassion, extending the same gentleness to others on their respective journeys. This compassionate outlook nurtures harmonious relationships, promotes forgiveness and reconciliation, and fosters a sense of unity within diverse communities. Through acts of compassion, we contribute to creating a world rooted in love, empathy, and mutual respect.

In the tapestry of human existence, spirituality weaves a thread that transcends boundaries of time, culture, and belief. It is a journey that beckons each of us to explore the depths of our inner being, seeking meaning, purpose, and connection beyond the tangible realms of everyday life. Throughout history and across civilizations, spirituality has been a guiding light for seekers, offering solace in times of turmoil, wisdom in moments of uncertainty, and a profound sense of unity amidst diversity.

At its essence, spirituality invites us to embark on a quest for self-discovery. Through practices such as meditation, prayer, and introspection, we peel away the layers of ego and superficial desires, delving into the core of our existence. It is here, in the quietude of our inner sanctuary, that we confront our deepest fears, aspirations, and truths. This journey of self-discovery is not merely introspective but transformative, as it unveils our interconnectedness with all life forms and the universe itself.

Spirituality also nurtures resilience in the face of life's adversities. It teaches us those challenges are not obstacles but opportunities for growth and evolution. Drawing from spiritual teachings, we learn to cultivate patience, acceptance, and equanimity, understanding that every experience—joyous or painful—has its place in the grand tapestry of our lives. This resilience empowers us to navigate the complexities of existence with grace and fortitude, knowing that we are supported by forces larger than ourselves.

Moreover, spirituality fosters compassion—both towards ourselves and others. It encourages us to embrace empathy and kindness, recognizing the inherent dignity and divinity in every being. This compassion forms the bedrock of harmonious relationships and societal cohesion, transcending differences of creed, race, or ideology. It is through compassion that we build bridges of understanding and forge a shared path towards a more inclusive and compassionate world.

The wisdom of spiritual traditions, such as the teachings of the Bhagavad Gita, the Quran, the Bible, or the teachings of spiritual leaders and mentors, provides timeless guidance on leading a purposeful and ethical life. These teachings illuminate the path of righteousness, emphasizing virtues like honesty, humility, and service to others. They remind us that true fulfilments lie not in material wealth or transient pleasures but in leading a life of integrity and moral courage.

As we reflect on the myriad facets of spirituality, we recognize its universal appeal and transformative power. It is a journey that transcends the confines of religious dogma, inviting individuals of all backgrounds to seek deeper meaning and fulfilments in their lives. Whether through prayer in a mosque, meditation in a monastery, or acts of kindness in our communities, spirituality offers a pathway to inner peace and harmony.

In closing, embracing spirituality is not merely a personal choice but a collective endeavour to nurture the inherent goodness within ourselves and humanity as a whole. It is a journey that unfolds in moments of quiet contemplation, in acts of selfless service, and in the boundless compassion we extend to others.

As we continue on this journey, may we find solace in the wisdom of spiritual traditions, strength in our shared humanity, and a profound sense of purpose in contributing to a more compassionate and enlightened world.

A Gratitude Note

Dear Readers,

As we conclude this journey through the realms of spirituality, I extend my heartfelt gratitude to each of you. Your openness to explore and embrace the wisdom shared here has been inspiring. Remember, as Rumi beautifully said,

> *"The wound is the place where the Light enters you."*

May these words resonate in your hearts as you continue your own spiritual journeys.

In the words of Thich Nhat Hanh,

> *"Sometimes your joy is the source of your smile, but sometimes your smile can be the source of your joy."*

Let us carry this spirit of joy and gratitude forward, nurturing our spirits and spreading kindness and compassion in our interactions.

Lastly, let us reflect on the words of Swami Vivekananda,

> *"Arise, awake, and stop not until the goal is reached."*

May each of us awaken to our true potential and continue to grow in wisdom, compassion, and inner peace.

With deepest gratitude and warmest wishes,
- Harish Tolani
(Chikoo Bhaiya)

www.ingramcontent.com/pod-product-compliance
Lightning Source LLC
LaVergne TN
LVHW041921070526
838199LV00051BA/2693